easy crochet
Weekend

easy crochet
Weekend

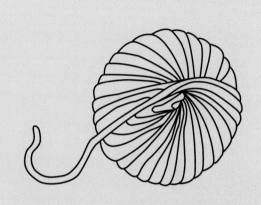

30 quick projects to make and wear

Consultant: Nikki Trench

KP CRAFT
Cincinnati, Ohio

Easy Crochet Weekend
30 Quick Projects to Make and Wear

First published in Great Britain in 2013 by Hamlyn.
 Published by KP Craft, an imprint of F+W Media,
Inc., 10151 Carver Road, Suite 200, Blue Ash, Ohio 45242.
(800) 289-0963

www.fwmedia.com

18   17   16   15   14   5   4   3   2   1

DISTRIBUTED IN CANADA BY FRASER DIRECT
100 Armstrong Avenue
Georgetown, ON, Canada L7G 5S4
Tel: (905) 877-4411

SRN: T2886
ISBN-13: 978-1-4402-4174-1

Contents

Introduction

Crochet is easy, and it grows fast. Master a few basic stitches (and the terminology) and you can create stylish crocheted items to wear, use to decorate your home, and as gifts for friends and family in next to no time and with minimal experience.

Whether you are a relative beginner, a confident convert, or a long-term aficionado, there are projects here to delight. While your first attempts may be a bit uneven, a little practice and experimentation will ensure you soon improve. None of the projects in this book is beyond the scope of even those fairly new to the hobby. Even the most basic of stitches can be translated into covetable items.

It is immensely satisfying to create something from scratch, and even more so when this is achieved in a short space of time. All the projects in this book, which range from stylish items you can wear—hats, scarves, and socks—through to practical accessories and trinkets such as a laptop bag and gift charms, can be completed over a weekend. All would make charming, unique gifts.

Crochet essentials

All you really need to get crocheting is a hook and some yarn. For many projects that's it, and where additional items are required, most of these can be found in a fairly basic sewing kit. All measurements are given in imperial and metric. Choose which to work in and stick with it since conversions may not be exact in all instances.

- **Hooks** Metrically sized hooks were used to make the projects in this book. Approximate equivalents in U.S. sizes are given in ( )s within the patterns; but you may need to experiment with different sizes to obtain the correct gauge (just as you might need to change hook sizes within one system). Metric hooks manufactured by Aero can be purchased from online suppliers.
- **Yarns** Specific yarns are given for each project, but if you want to make substitutions, full details of the

yarn's composition and the ball lengths are given so that you can choose alternatives, either from online sources, or your local supplier, many of whom have very knowledgeable staff. Do keep any leftover yarns (not forgetting the ball bands, since these contain vital information) to use for future projects. The initials DK stand for "double knitting," a standard weight of British yarn, slightly thinner than a worsted weight and slightly thicker than a sport weight. A "4-ply" yarn is about half the weight of a DK yarn. An "Aran-weight" yarn is roughly equivalent to a worsted weight. These yarns are now becoming more widely available in the U.S.

- **Additional items** Some of the projects require making up and finishing, and need further materials and equipment, such as needles (both ordinary and round-pointed tapestry ones) and thread, buttons, ribbons and other accessories. These are detailed for each project in the Getting Started box.

What is in this book

All projects are illustrated with several photographs to show you the detail of the work—both inspirational and useful for reference. A full summary of each project is given in the Getting Started box so you can see exactly what's involved. Here, projects are graded from one star (straightforward, suitable for beginners) through two (more challenging), to three stars (for crocheters with more confidence and experience).

Also in the Getting Started box is the size of each finished item, yarn(s) and additional materials needed, and what tension the project is worked in. Finally, a breakdown of the steps involved is given so you know exactly what the project entails before you start.

At the start of the pattern instructions is a key to all abbreviations particular to the project and occasional notes expand if necessary.

Additional information

Occasionally, more information is needed, or a slightly specialist technique is used. Magic circles, for example, feature several times, and detailed instructions for how to make them are given as a note on page 21.

Multicolor pillows

Choose a mixture of colors and styles to give your sofa the designer look.

Mix 'n' match styles with this set of zingy pillows. There is a small textured rib-patterned pillow with an envelope fastening, mid-sized lacy pillows featuring contrasting linings and zipper fastenings, and a large striped pillow, also with an envelope fastening.

The Yarn

Debbie Bliss Stella (approx. 96 yards/88m per 50g/1¾oz ball) is a luxurious mix of 60% silk, 20% rayon, and 20% cotton in a bulky weight, so it works up quickly. It can be machine washed at a low temperature, and the color palette has natural shades and bright ones.

GETTING STARTED

Ribbed and striped pillows are simple double crochet fabrics and the lace pattern is easy.

Size:
Ribbed pillow measures 12 inches (30cm) square
Lace pillow measures 16 inches (40cm) square
Striped pillow measures 20 inches (50cm) square

How much yarn:
Ribbed 4 x 50g (1¾oz) balls of Debbie Bliss Stella in Bright Pink (shade 08)
Lace 4 x 50g (1¾oz) balls of Debbie Bliss Stella in Lime (shade 15) or Orange (shade 06)
Striped 4 x 50g (1¾oz) balls of Debbie Bliss Stella in each of color A—Turquoise (shade 12) and color B—Pale Blue (shade 11)

Hook:
5.50mm (I/9) crochet hook

Additional items:
Ribbed 3 large buttons, 12 inches (30cm) square pillow form. Lace 16½ x 32 inches (42 x 82cm) cotton lining fabric, 16-inch (40cm) zipper, sewing thread, 16 inch (40cm) square pillow form. Striped 4 large buttons, 20 inch (50cm) square pillow form

Gauge:
Ribbed 13 sts and 9 rows measure 4 inches (10cm) square Lace 15 sts and 7 rows measure 4 inches (10cm) square Striped 13sts and 7 rows measure 4 inches (10cm) square; for all pillows over patt using 5.50mm (I/9) hook
IT IS ESSENTIAL TO WORK TO THE STATED GAUGE TO ACHIEVE SUCCESS.

What you have to do:
Ribbed Work throughout in double crochet with relief doubles to form vertical "ribs." Work buttonhole border in single crochet. Construct envelope opening with button fastenings. Lace Work simple lace pattern. Make up lining and sew in zipper. Striped Work in double crochet changing color every 2 rows. Work buttonhole border in single crochet. Construct envelope opening.

Instructions

Abbreviations:

beg = beginning
ch = chain(s)
cm = centimeter(s)
dc = double crochet
dc/rb = relief double crochet back
dc/rf = relief double crochet front
mm = millimeters
patt = pattern
rep = repeat
RS = right side
sc = single crochet
st(s) = stitch(es)
st(s) = stitch(es)
V-st = work 1dc, ch1 and 1dc
WS = wrong side
yo = yarn over hook

RIBBED PILLOW

(Worked in one piece)
Ch 42.

Foundation row: (RS) 1dc into 4th ch from hook, 1dc into each ch to end, turn. 40dc.

Row 1: ch2 (counts as first dc), skip 1dc, 1dc into each of next 3dc, *into each of next 2dc work: yo, insert hook from right to left through stem of next st on back of work, pull loop through and complete dc as usual—called dc/rb, 1dc into each of next 4dc, rep from * to end, working last dc into top of turning ch, turn.

Row 2: ch2, skip 1dc, 1dc into each of next 3dc, *into each of next 2dc work: yo, insert hook from right to left through stem of next st on front of work, pull loop through and complete dc as usual—called dc/rb, 1dc into each of next 4dc, rep from * to end, working last dc into top of turning ch, turn.

The last 2 rows form pat. Rep them until work measures 27½in (70cm) from beg,

ending with a Row 2.

Buttonhole border:

Row 1: ch1 (counts as first sc), skip 1dc, 1sc into each dc to end, working last sc into top of turning ch, turn.

Row 2: ch1, skip 1sc, 1sc into each of next 6sc, (ch2, skip 2sc, 1sc into each of next 10sc) twice, ch2, skip 2sc, 1sc into each st to end, turn.

Row 3: ch1, skip 1sc, 1sc into each sc to end, working 2sc into each ch2 space for buttonhole. Fasten off.

LACE PILLOWS
Back:

Ch 58.

Foundation row: (RS) V-st into 5th ch from hook, *skip 2ch, V-st into next ch, rep from * to last 2ch, skip 1ch, 1dc into last ch, turn.

Row 1: ch3 (counts as first dc), *skip 2 sts, 3dc into 1-ch sp on next V-st, rep from * to end, working last dc into top of turning ch, turn.

Row 2: ch3, *skip 2dc, V-st into next dc (center st of 3dc worked on previous row), rep from * to last st, skip this st, 1dc into turning ch, turn. The last 2 rows form patt. Rep them until work measures 16 inches (40cm) from beg. Fasten off.

Front:

Work as given for Back.

STRIPED PILLOW

(Worked in one piece)

Ch67.

Foundation row: (RS) 1dc into 4ch ch from hook, 1dc into each dc to end, turn. 65 sts.

Row 1: ch3 (counts as first dc), skip 1dc, 1dc into each dc to end, work last dc into top of turning ch, turn. Rep last row to form pat, working in stripes of 2 rows each B and A until 38 stripes in all have been completed and ending with 2 rows in B.

Buttonhole border:

Row 1: With A, ch1 (counts as first sc), skip 1dc, 1sc into each dc to end, working last sc into top of turning ch, turn.

Row 2: ch1, skip 1sc, 1sc into each of next 11dc, (ch2, skip 2sc, 1sc into each of next 11sc) 3 times, 2ch, skip 2sc, 1sc into each st to end, turn.

Row 3: ch1, skip 1sc, 1sc into each sc to end, working 2sc into each 2ch space for buttonhole. Fasten off.

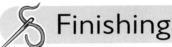 Finishing

RIBBED PILLOW

Place cover WS down with buttonhole border at top edge and fold over 4¼ inches (11cm) at top edge. Now bring lower edge up over top of flap so that edge is level with top fold. (The cover should measure 12 x 12 inches (30 x 30cm) so adjust folds if necessary.) Join side seams, working through all thicknesses at flap. Turn RS out and sew on buttons to match buttonholes.

LACE PILLOWS

Turn and press ⅜in (1cm) to WS along short ends of lining fabric and insert zipper into this edge. Open zipper and turn lining WS out. With RS facing and zipper at one edge, fold at the other, stitch lining free edges together taking ⅜in (1cm) seam. Press flat and turn lining RS out through zipper opening.

Join top and side seams on front and back panels. Slide lining into crochet cover. Using sewing thread, slipstitch lower open edge in place to lining on either side of zipper. Insert pillow form and close zipper.

STRIPED PILLOW

Place cover WS down with buttonhole border at top edge and fold over border plus 9 rows at top edge so that stripes match at side edges. Now bring lower edge up over top of flap so that edge is level with top fold and stripes match at side edges. (The cover should measure 20 x 20 inches/50 x 50cm.) Join side seams, working through all thicknesses at flap. Turn RS out and sew on buttons to match buttonholes.

Pull-on hat

Two contrasting patterns are used for this striking and feminine beanie.

This beanie is worked in the round, with a dense fabric of basic stitches for the crown, and edged with a deep band of pretty lacy shells worked in two colors.

GETTING STARTED

★★ *Working in rounds may be unfamiliar at first. Pay attention to the shaping.*

Size:

To fit head: *20[22:24]in (51[56:61]cm) in circumference*

Note: *Figures in brackets [ ] refer to larger sizes; where there is only one set of figures, it applies to all sizes*

How much yarn:

1[1:2] x 50g (1¾oz) balls of Patons Diploma Gold DK in color A—Cream (shade 6142)

1[1:1] ball in color B—New Berry (shade 6239)

Hooks:

3.75mm (F/5) crochet hook

4.00mm (G/6) crochet hook

Gauge:

First 4 rounds measure 3 inches (7.5cm) in diameter worked on 4.00mm (G/6) hook

IT IS ESSENTIAL TO WORK TO THE STATED GAUGE TO ACHIEVE SUCCESS.

What you have to do:

Make 5 chains for center of crown and slip stitch into first chain to form a circle. Work crown in one color and alternating rounds of single and double crochet, increasing at regular intervals to shape hat. Join in a second color and work shell edging in rounds, alternating the two colors on each round.

The Yarn

Patons Diploma Gold DK (approx. 136 yards/120m per 50g/1¾oz ball) is a practical mix of 55% wool, 25% acrylic, and 20% nylon. It is machine washable in plenty of shades.

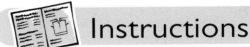 ## Instructions

With larger hook and A, ch5, join into a circle with a sl st into first ch.

Round 1: (Working into circle and over starting tail of yarn at same time), ch1 (counts as first sc), 11sc into ring, join with a sl st into first ch. 12sc.

Round 2: ch3 (counts as first dc), 2dc into each of 11sc, 1dc into last sc, join with a sl st into 3rd of 3ch. 24tr.

Round 3: ch1, (1sc into next dc, 2sc into next dc) 11 times, 1sc into each of last 2dc, join with a sl st into first ch. 36sc.

Round 4: ch3, (1dc into each of next 2sc, 2dc into next sc) 11 times, 1dc into each of last 3sc, join with a sl st into 3rd of 3ch. 48dc.

Round 5: ch1, (1sc into each of next 5dc, 2sc into next dc) 7 times, 1sc into each of next 6dc, join with a sl st into first ch. 56sc.

Round 6: ch3, (1dc into each of next 6sc, 2dc into next

Abbreviations:

beg = beginning
ch = chain(s)
cm = centimeter(s)
dc = double crochet
mm = millimeter(s)
rep = repeat
sc = single crochet
sl st = slip stitch
sp = space
st(s) = stitch(es)

sc) 7 times, 1dc into each of next 7sc, join with a sl st into 3rd of 3ch. 64dc.

Round 7: ch1, skip first dc, 1sc into each dc, join with a sl st into first ch.

Round 8: ch3, (1dc into each of next 7sc, 2dc into next sc) 7 times, 1dc into each of next 8sc, join with a sl st into 3rd of 3ch. 72dc.

Round 9: As Round 7.

Round 10: ch3, (1dc into each of next 8sc, 2dc into next sc) 7 times, 1dc into each of next 9sc, join with a sl st into 3rd of 3ch. 80dc.

Round 11: As Round 7.

2nd and 3rd sizes only:

Round 12: ch3, (1dc into each of next 9sc, 2dc into next sc) 7 times, 1dc into each of next 10sc, join with a sl st into 3rd of 3ch. 88dc.

Round 13: As Round 7.

3rd size only:

Round 14: ch3, (1dc into each of next 10sc, 2dc into next sc) 7 times, 1dc into each of next 11sc, join with a sl st into 3rd of 3ch. 96dc.

Round 15: As Round 7.

All sizes:

80[88:96] sts.

Next round: ch3, skip first sc, 1dc into each sc, join with a sl st into 3rd of 3ch.

Next round: As Round 7.

Rep last 2 rounds until hat measures 5[5½:6]in (12.5[14:15]cm) from center to outside edge, ending with a round of sc and changing to B for final sl st of last round.

Note: Do not fasten off yarn after each round, but strand it up inside the hat.

Round 1: With B, ch4, 2dc into first sc, *skip 3sc, (2dc, ch1, 2dc) into next sc, rep from * ending with 1dc into same place as base of 4ch, change to A, join with a sl st into 3rd of 4ch.

Round 2: With A, sl st into 1ch sp, ch4, 2dc into same sp, *skip 4dc, (2dc, ch1, 2dc) into 1-ch sp, rep from * ending with 1dc into same sp as beg of round, change to B, join with a sl st into 3rd of 4ch.

HOW TO
WORK IN THE ROUND

Instead of working in rows you can work crochet by starting with a central ring and continuing outward in rounds. The right side of the work will be facing you all the time as you work.

1 Begin by working the specified number of chains; join the first to the last with a slip stitch (or make a magic circle, see Note page 21). Hold the bottom of the loop between your thumb and forefinger and make the starting chain.

3 To close the round, work a slip stitch into the top of the starting chain.

5 Continue in this way, working each round and joining the rounds with a slip stitch into the starting chain.

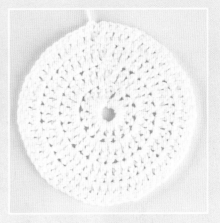

2 Work the first round directly into the loop ring.

4 Make the required starting chain and then continue working the next round making each stitch as instructed by working under both loops of the stitch in the round below.

6 Working each round as instructed, the number of stitches in each round is increased so that the circle of stitches grows in size.

Round 3: With B, work as Round 2, changing to A for final sl st.
Rep last 2 rounds twice more. Fasten off B.

Change to smaller hook.
Next round: With A, sl st into 1ch sp, ch4, 1sc into same sp, *ch1, skip 2dc, 1sc into sp between 2 groups of dc, ch1, skip 2dc, (1sc, ch3, 1sc) into next 1ch sp, rep from * ending with ch1, skip 2dc, 1sc into sp between 2 groups of dc, ch1, join with a sl st into first ch. Fasten off.

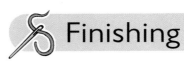

Finishing

Darn in all yarn ends. Press lightly according to directions on yarn label.

Giant scarf

Worked in thick yarn on a large hook, this long scarf is made in no time!

Made extra long for winding around your neck, this fabulous scarf has an eye-catching large openwork pattern and long fringe.

GETTING STARTED

★★ *Although bulky yarn works up quickly, the pattern needs concentration.*

Size:
Scarf measures 9½ x 80 inches (24 x 204cm), excluding fringe

How much yarn:
9 x 50g (1¾oz) balls of Debbie Bliss Como in Rose Pink (shade 10)

Hook:
9.00mm (M/13) crochet hook

Gauge:
9 sts (1 patt rep) measure 4¼ inches (11cm) and 4 rows (1 patt rep) measure 3 inches (7.5cm) on 9.00mm (M/13) hook
IT IS ESSENTIAL TO WORK TO THE STATED GAUGE TO ACHIEVE SUCCESS.

What you have to do:
Make long length of chain for foundation chain. Work foundation row and last row (long side edges) in single crochet. Work 3 repeats of motif pattern with large clusters and chain spaces. Work two rows of single crochet along short ends. Add tassels to short ends of scarf.

The Yarn

Debbie Bliss Como (approx. 42m/46 yards per 50g/1¾oz ball) is a luxurious blend of 90% wool and 10% cashmere in a bulky weight. It is softly spun and looks good in large, distinctive patterns such as this. The colors are mainly subtle shades.

Instructions

Abbreviations:

ch = chain(s)
cl = cluster(s)
cm = centimeter(s)
cont = continue
dc = double crochet
mm = millimeter(s)
patt = pattern
rep = repeat
RS = right side
sc = single crochet
sl st = slip stitch
sp = space(s)
st(s) = stitch(es)
yo = yarn over hook

SCARF:

Ch168.

Foundation row: (RS) 1sc into 2nd ch from hook, 1sc into each ch to end, turn. 167sc.

Row 1: ch3 (counts as first dc), work 2dc into first st leaving last loop of each on hook, yo and draw through all 3 loops on hook—called 2dc cl, *skip 3 sts, 2dc cl in next st, ch3, sl st into same st as last cl, ch5, skip 4 sts, sl st into next st, ch3, 2dc cl into same st as sl st, rep from * to last 4 sts, skip 3 sts, 2dc cl into last st, ch3, sl st into same st as cl, turn.

Row 2: ch3, *work 3dc in top of next cl leaving last loop of each on hook, yo and draw through all 4 loops on hook—called 3dc cl, ch3, 3dc cl in same place as last 3dc cl, ch2, sl st into 3rd of 5ch, ch2, rep from * ending last rep with (3dc cl, ch3, 3dc cl) into top of next cl, turn.

Row 3: ch1, *5sc into 3ch sp between cl of previous row, ch4, rep from * ending last rep with 5sc into last 3-ch sp, turn.

Row 4: ch1, *1sc into each of next 5 sts, 4sc into 4-ch sp, rep from * ending 1sc into each of last 5 sts, turn.

Rep last 4 rows twice more. Fasten off.

With RS of work facing, rejoin yarn to one short end of Scarf and work 17sc along row ends. Work 1 more row in sc. Fasten off. Complete other short end of Scarf in same way.

Tassels:

Cut 5 x 14-inch (35cm) lengths of yarn for each tassel. Knot 5 tassels across each short end of Scarf. Trim tassels evenly.

Pretend Pastries

Serve up a teatime treat with these funky crochet cakes.

Traditional British teatime favorites—without the calories—make an amusing decoration for the table.

GETTING STARTED

 Easy stitches, but care is needed with construction.

Size:

Slice of Victoria sponge (layer cake): 4¾in (12cm) tall x 4¼in (11cm) long x 2¾in (7cm) at widest point

Custard slice: 1¾in (4.5cm) x 4 inches (10cm) x 1¾in (4.5cm) deep

Slice of Battenberg: 3½in (9cm) square x 1in (2.5cm) deep

Apricot Danish pastry: 4 inches (10cm) square x 1⅜in (3.5cm) deep

Cherry Bakewell Tart: 3⅛in (8cm) in diameter x 2 inches (5cm) deep

Note: All measurements are approximate

How much yarn:

For all 5 pastries:

1 x 100g (3½oz) ball of Patons Fab DK in each of 3 colors: A—Beige (shade 02331); B—Cream (shade 02307) and C—White (shade 02306)

1 x 25g (1oz) ball of Patons FaB DK in each of six colors: D—Red (shade 02322); E—Camel (shade 02308); F—Brown (shade 02309); G—Pink (shade 02304); H—Lemon (shade 02330) and I—Canary (shade 02305)

Hook:

4.00mm (G/6) crochet hook

Additional items:

Stitch markers

Foam block for cutting to shape

Polyester fiberfill

Gauge:

20 sts and 22 rows measure 4 inches (10cm) square over sc on 4.00mm (G/6) hook

What you have to do:

Work individual pastries in colors specified and mainly simple stitches, including single, half double, and double crochet. Work in rows or rounds as specified. Follow instructions for simple increasing or decreasing to shape pastries. Construct pastries following instructions, adding block of foam or polyester fiberfill.

The Yarn

Patons FaB DK is 100% acrylic. Popular shades come in 100g (3½oz) balls (approx. 274m/299 yards per ball); plenty of colors come in 25g (1oz) balls (approx. 68m/74 yards per ball).

Instructions

VICTORIA SPONGE SLICE:

Outer cake piece:

With A, ch4.

Row 1: 3dc in 4th ch from hook, turn. 4 sts.

Row 2: ch3 (counts as first dc), 1dc in st at base of ch, 1dc in each st to end, working last dc in 3rd of 3ch, turn. 1 st inc at beg of row.

Rows 3–10: As Row 2. 13 sts.

Row 11: ch3, skip st at base of ch, 1dc in front loop only of each st to end, turn.

Row 12: ch3, skip st at base of ch, 1dc in each st to end, joining in D on last st, turn.

Row 13: With D, ch2, skip st at base of ch, 1hdc in each st to end, joining in C on last st, turn. Cut off D.

Row 14: With C, ch2, skip st at base of ch, 1hdc in front loop only of each st to end, changing to A on last st, turn. Cut off C.

Row 15: With A, as Row 11.

Row 16: Work in dc.

Row 17: ch3, skip st at base of ch, 1dc in front loop only of each of next 10 sts, dc2tog over last st and top of turning ch, turn. 1 st dec at end of row.

Row 18: ch3, skip st at base of ch, 1dc into each st to last 2 sts, dc2tog over last st and top of turning ch, turn. 1 st dec at end of row.

Rows 19–25: As Row 18. 4 sts.

Row 26: ch3, skip st at base of ch, dc3tog. Fasten off.

Cake sides piece:

With B, ch45.

Row 1: 1dc in 4th ch from hook, 1dc in each ch to end, turn. 43 sts.

Row 2: ch2 (counts as first hdc), skip st at base of ch, 1hdc in each st to end, working last hdc in top of turning ch and joining in D on last st, turn.

Row 3: With D, work in hdc, joining in C on last st. Cut off D.

Row 4: With C, work 1hdc in front loop only of each st, changing to B on last st, Cut off C.

Row 5: With B, work 1hdc in front loop only of each st to end, turn.

Row 6: ch3, skip st at base of ch, work in dc to end. Fasten off.

Cream swirl:

With C, make a magic circle (see Note right), completing as foll:

Round 1: (Ch10, 1sc) 9 times into circle, ch6. Fasten off, working yarn, leaving a long end.

Pull gently on starting yarn end to tighten circle and close hole. Thread tail in tapestry needle, then take yarn through 5th ch of each loop and back through top of 6ch. Draw yarn up until loops gather towards center but leaving an internal circle of about ¾in (2cm). Turn swirl upside down to assess size and tighten or loosen yarn accordingly. Make knot to fasten off but leave yarn tail for attaching decoration to cake.

Strawberry:

With D, make a magic circle(see Note right), completing as foll:

Round 1: ch1, work 6sc in circle, join with a sl st in first sc. If using st marker, start marking beg of each round.

Round 2: (2sc in next st, 1sc in each of next 2 sts) to end. 8 sts.

Round 3: (2sc in next st, 1sc in each of next 3 sts) to end. 10 sts.

Round 4: (2sc in next st, 1sc in each of next 4 sts) to end. 12 sts.

Round 5: As Round 3. 15 sts.

Round 6: As Round 2. 20 sts.

Round 7: As Round 4. 24 sts.

Round 8: (Sc2tog over next 2 sts, 1sc in next st) to end. 16 sts.

Round 9: (Sc2tog over next 2 sts) to end. 8 sts. Fasten off. Turn inside out, stuff, then gather up yarn around edge of opening, draw up tight and fasten off. Use C to embroider small seeds on strawberry.

CUSTARD SLICE:
Top and bottom rectangles:

(make 2)

With B, ch10.

Row 1: 1dc in 4th ch from hook, 1dc in each ch to end, turn. 8 sts.

Abbreviations:

beg = beginning;

ch = chain(s);

cm = centimeter(s)

dc = double crochet;

dc2(3)tog = work 1dc in each of next 2(3) sts leaving last loop of each of hook, yo and draw through all 3(4) loops

dec = decrease;

foll = follows;

hdc = half double crochet

in = inch(es)

inc = increased

mm = millimeter(s)

rdcb = relief double back as foll: yo, insert hook from right to left and from back around stem of next st, yo and complete dc in usual way;

rem = remaining;

rep = repeat

sc = single crochet;

sc2tog = (insert hook in next st, yo and draw a loop through) twice, yo and draw through all 3 loops on hook;

sl st = slip stitch;

st(s) = stitch(es)

yo = yarn over hook

Note: To make a Magic Circle, wrap yarn clockwise around forefinger twice to form a ring. Holding end of yarn between thumb and middle finger, insert hook into ring and draw yarn from ball through.

Rows 2–9: ch3 (counts as first dc), skip st at base of ch, 1dc in each st to end, working last dc in 3rd of 3ch, turn. Fasten off.

Long side strip:

With B, 53ch.

Row 1: 1hdc in 3rd ch from hook, 1hdc in each ch to end, turn. 52 sts.

Row 2: ch2 (counts as first hdc), skip st at base of ch, 1hdc in each st to end, working last hdc in 2nd of 2ch. Fasten off.

Pastry layers: (make 2 with E and 1 with A)

Work as given for top and bottom rectangles.

Icing layer:

With C, make ch10.

Row 1: (RS) 1dc in 4th ch from hook, 1dc in each ch to end, joining in F on last st, turn. 8 sts. Cut off C.

Row 2: With F, ch1 (counts as first sc), skip st at base of ch, 1sc in each of next 3 sts, 1rdcb around next st, 1sc in each of next 3 sts, joining in C on last st, turn. Cut off F.

Row 3: With C, ch3, skip st at base of ch, 1dc in each st to end, joining in F on last st, turn. Cut off C.

Rows 4–11: Rep Rows 2 and 3 4 more times. Fasten off.

BATTENBERG SLICE:

Cake top: (make 2 with G and 2 with H)

Ch9.

Row 1: 1sc in 2nd ch from hook, 1sc in each ch to end, turn. 8 sts.

Rows 2–8: ch1 (counts as first sc), skip st at base of ch, 1sc in each st to end, turn. Fasten off.

Cake base:

With B, ch17. Work 16 rows in sc on 16 sts as given for cake top. Fasten off.

Cake side:

With B, ch5. Work 64 rows in sc on 4 sts as given for cake top. Fasten off.

APRICOT DANISH PASTRY:

Pastry inner layer:

With B, ch23.

Row 1: 1dc in 4th ch from hook, 1dc in each ch to end, turn. 21 sts.

Row 2: ch3 (counts as first dc), skip st at base of ch, 1dc in each st to end, working last dc in 3rd of 3ch, turn.

Rows 3–11: As Row 2. Fasten off.

Pastry outer layer:

With A, ch23. Work 11 rows in dc as given for inner layer, joining in E at end of last row. Cut off A.

Edging:

With E, ch2, work in hdc around outer edges of square, working 2hdc in each corner st, join with a sl st in 2nd of 2ch. Fasten off.

Apricot half:

With I, make a magic circle (see Note page 21), completing as foll:

Round 1: ch1, work 6sc in circle, join with a sl st in first sc. If using st marker, start marking beg of each round.

Round 2: 2sc in each st to end. 12 sts.

Round 3: (2sc in next st, 1sc in next st) to end. 18 sts.

Round 4: Work in sc.

Round 5: (2sc in next st, 1sc in each of next 2 sts) to end. 24 sts.

Round 6: Work in sc.

Round 7: (Dc2tog over next 2 sts) to end. 12 sts. Lightly stuff apricot half to make a flattish dome.

Round 8: As Round 7. 6 sts. Fasten off.

Icing drizzle:

With C, ch80. Fasten off.

CHERRY BAKEWELL:
Tart top top:
With C, make a magic circle (see Note page 21), completing as foll:

Round 1: ch1, work 7sc in circle, join with a sl st in first sc. If using st marker, start marking beg of each round.
Round 2: 2sc in each st to end. 14 sts.
Round 3: (2sc in next st, 1sc in next st) to end. 21 sts.
Round 4: (2sc in next st, 1sc in each of next 2 sts) to end. 28 sts.
Round 5: (2sc in next st, 1sc in each of next 3 sts) to end. 35 sts.
Round 6: (2sc in next st, 1sc in each of next 4 sts) to end. 42 sts.
Round 7: (2sc in next st, 1sc in each of next 5 sts) to end. 49 sts.
Round 8: Work in sc. Fasten off.
Cherry:
With D, make a magic circle (see Note page 21), completing as foll:

Round 1: ch1, work 6sc in circle, join with a sl st in first sc. If using st marker, start marking beg of each round.
Round 2: (2sc in next st, 1sc in next st) to end. 9 sts.
Round 3: (2sc in next st, 1sc in each of next 2 sts) to end. 12 sts. Fasten off, leaving a long end. Sew cherry to center of tart top.
Base:
(Worked with WS facing)
With A, work as given for tart top until Round 7 has been completed. 49 sts.
Round 8: ch1, sl st into each st to end.
Round 9: (Working into front loop only of each st in this round, sc2tog, 1sc in each of next 5 sts) to end. 42 sts.
Rounds 10–12: Work in sc.
Round 13: (2sc in next st, 1sc in each of next 5 sts) to end. 49 sts.
Join to tart top:
Next round: Place tart top in center of base, inserting hook through st on edge of tart top and next st along base work 1sc, matching up tart top and base, cont to work 1sc through pairs of sts until 30 sts have been worked; stuff tart with polyester filling, then complete rem pairs of sts to close gap.
Edging:
Next round: Sl st in next st, (2sc in next st, sl st in next st) to end. Fasten off.

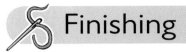

Finishing

VICTORIA SPONGE SLICE:
Fold cake sides piece in half and mark center. Align short ends with back of outer cake piece, using red and white stripes as a guide. Pin, then sew matched-up edges in place. Match points at start and end of outer cake piece to marker at center of cake sides piece and pin edges in place. Sew 3 of the 4 edges. Either cut a foam wedge to shape or stuff firmly with polyester filling. Join rem edge. With D, sew strawberry to cream swirl, then use yarn tail of C to sew decoration to top of cake.

VANILLA SLICE:
Join ends of long side strip, then sew one edge around bottom rectangle. Cut foam block to fit, or stuff firmly with polyester filling, then sew top rectangle to other side of long strip. Sew a pastry layer in E, then another in A on bottom rectangle. Sew a pastry layer in E, then icing layer on top rectangle.

BATTENBURG SLICE:
Using picture as a guide and G, sew 4 small squares of cake top together. Join short ends of cake side together, then fold in half (with join at one side) and then in half again and mark quarter points with pins. Matching quarter points to corners of base square, sew cake side in place. Then sew cake top in place around 3 sides, leaving one side open. Stuff cake firmly with polyester filling or cut foam block to fit, then neatly slipstitch last side closed.

APRICOT DANISH PASTRY:
Place pastry inner layer on top of outer layer. Place apricot half in center of squares as a guide, then fold in four corners of squares to middle just under edge of apricot and sew corners in place. Attach apricot half to center of folded squares, making sure that stitches do not show through onto bottom of pastry. Place icing drizzle as desired and sew in place. "Puff" up pastry by cupping cake in hands to bring up edges slightly.

Fingerless mitts

Crochet this fashionable accessory: mitts that
can be worn with your favorite jacket or coat.

These long, fingerless mitts in a straightforward, slightly openwork, pattern have cuffs worked in relief double crochet with ribbed appearance.

GETTING STARTED

★★ *Pattern is not too difficult, as there are no fingers to shape, but it does require concentration for thumb shaping.*

Size:
To fit an adult woman's hand

How much yarn:
2 x 50g (1 ¾oz) balls of Debbie Bliss Rialto DK in Purple (shade 16)

Hook:
4.00mm (G/6) crochet hook

Gauge:
16 sts and 12 rows measure 4 inches (10cm) square over main patt on 4.00mm (G/6) hook
IT IS ESSENTIAL TO WORK TO THE STATED GAUGE TO ACHIEVE SUCCESS.

What you have to do:
Make foundation chain and join into a circle. Work foundation round of double crochet. Work "cuff" in mock ribbing comsisting of relief double crochet. Work main pattern of V stitches, shaping for thumb as instructed. Leave stitches for thumb and continue main part, finishing with single crochet edging. Return to thumb stitches and complete thumb.

The Yarn
Debbie Bliss Rialto DK (approx. 105m/114 yards per 50g/1¾oz ball) contains 100% merino wool. This yarn is soft and warm, and can be machine washed at a low temperature, so is perfect for these mitts. There are plenty of great shades to choose from.

Instructions

Abbreviations:

beg = beginning
ch = chain(s)
cm = centimeter(s)
cont = continue
dc = double crochet
dc/rb(f) = relief double crochet back(front)
foll = follows
patt = pattern
rep = repeat
RS = right side
sc = single crochet
sl st = slip stitch
sp = space
st(s) = stitch(es)
WS = wrong side
yo = yarn over hook

RIGHT MITT:

Ch40, sl st into first ch to form a circle.

Foundation round: (WS) ch3, skip first ch, 1dc into each ch to end, join with a sl st into 3rd of 3ch at beg of round, turn. 40 sts.

Round 1: ch2 (counts as first dc), *yo, insert hook from in front and right to left around stem of next st and complete dc in normal way—called 1dc/rf, yo, insert hook from behind and from right to left around stem of next st and complete dc in normal way—called 1dc/rb, rep from * to last st, 1dc/rf around stem of last st, join with a sl st into 2nd of 2ch, turn.

Round 2: ch2 (counts as first dc), *1dc/rb around stem of next st, 1dc/rf around stem of next st, rep from * to last st, 1dc/rb around stem of last st, join with a sl st into 2nd of 2ch, turn.

Rep Rounds 1 and 2 twice more, then work Round 1 again, do not turn at end of last round.

Dec round: ch1 (counts as first sc), skip next st, 1sc into next st, (1sc into next st, skip next st, 1sc into next st) 6 times, skip next st, (1sc into next st, skip next st, 1sc into next st) 6 times, join with a sl st into first ch, do not turn. 26 sts.

Cont in main patt as foll:

Round 1: (RS) ch3, 1dc into st at base of 3ch, *skip next st, 2dc into next st—called V st, rep from * to end, join with a sl st into 3rd of 3ch, turn.

Round 2: Sl st into center of V st, ch3, 1dc into same V st, *2dc into center of next V st, rep from * to end, join with a sl st into 3rd of 3ch, turn.

Rep last round 6 more times. **

Shape for thumb:

Next round: (RS) Patt 16 sts, work 2dc into sp between last V st and next V st (inc made), patt rem 10 sts, join with a sl st into 3rd of 3ch, turn. 28 sts.

Next round: Patt 10 sts, work 2dc into sp between last V st and next V st, work 2dc into center of next V st, work 2dc into sp between last V st and next V st, patt rem 16 sts, join with a sl st into 3rd of 3ch, turn. 32 sts.

Next round: Patt 18 sts, work 2dc into sp between last V st and next V st, work 2dc into center of next V st, work 2dc into sp between last V st and next V st, patt rem 12 sts, join with a sl st into 3rd of 3ch, turn. 36 sts.

Patt 6 rounds straight.

Next round: (WS) Patt 10 sts, leave next 10 sts for thumb, patt rem 16 sts, join with a sl st into 3rd of 3ch, turn. 26 sts. Cont on these 26 sts only, patt 3 rounds.

Next round: ch1, 1sc into each st to end, join with a sl st into first ch, turn. Work 1 round in sc. Fasten off.

Thumb:

Rejoin yarn to 10 sts left for thumb. Work 1 round in main patt, then 2 rounds in sc. Fasten off.

LEFT MITT:

Work as given for Right Mitt to **.

Shape for thumb:

Next round: (RS) Patt 10 sts, work 2dc into sp between last V st and next V st (inc made), patt rem 16 sts, join with a sl st into 3rd of 3ch, turn. 28 sts.

Next round: Patt 16 sts, work 2dc into sp between last V st and next V st, work 2dc into center of next V st, work 2dc into sp between last V st and next V st, patt rem 10 sts, join with a sl st into 3rd of 3ch, turn. 32 sts.

Next round: Patt 12 sts, work 2dc into sp between last V st and next V st, work 2dc into center of next V st, work 2dc into sp between last V st and next V st, patt rem 18 sts, join with a sl st into 3rd of 3ch, turn. 36 sts.

Patt 6 rounds straight.

Next round: (WS) Patt 16 sts, leave next 10 sts for thumb, patt rem 10 sts, join with a sl st into 3rd of 3ch, turn. 26 sts. Cont on these 26 sts only, patt 3 rounds.

Next round: ch1, 1sc into each st to end, join with a sl st into first ch, turn. Work 1 round in sc. Fasten off.

Thumb:

Rejoin yarn to 10 sts left for thumb.
Work 1 round in main patt, then 2 rounds in sc. Fasten off.

Square-top hat

Equally at home on the streets, at the beach or in the country, this hat will become a firm favorite.

With its square crown of textured stitches and smooth sides worked in double crochet rounds, this handy hat will prove popular with the man in your life also.

The Yarn
Debbie Bliss Rialto DK (approx. 105m/114 yards per 50g/1¾oz ball) contains 100% merino wool. This luxurious yarn produces an attractive fabric, machine-washable at a low temperature, and you can choose from a wide color palette.

GETTING STARTED

 Working relief stitches requires concentration.

Size:
To fit an average-sized woman's head; circumference approximately 21 inches (53cm)

How much yarn:
2 x 50g (1¾oz) balls of Debbie Bliss Rialto DK in Teal Blue (shade 39)

Hooks:
3.50mm (E/4) crochet hook
4.00mm (G/6) crochet hook

Gauge:
18 sts and 10 rows measure 4 inches (10cm) square over rounds of dc on 4.00mm (G/6) hook
IT IS ESSENTIAL TO WORK TO THE STATED GAUGE TO ACHIEVE SUCCESS.

What you have to do:
Working in rounds of relief triples, start at center of crown and work a square. Continue in rounds of double crochet, without further increasing, for sides of hat. Finish with a border of relief double crochet to form a mock rib band.

Instructions

Abbreviations:

ch = chain
cm = centimeter(s)
dc = double crochet
foll = following
mm = centimeter(s)
rdcb = relief tr back: inserting hook from right to left and from back to front, work 1dc around stem of st indicated
rdcb2tog =work 1 rdcb around stem of sts indicated, leaving last loop of each on hook, yo and draw through all 3 loops
rdcf = relief dr front: inserting hook from right to left and from front to back, work 1dc around stem of st indicated
rep = repeat
rtrf = relief tr front: inserting hook from right to left and from front to back, work 1tr around stem of st indicated
sl st = slip stitch
sp = space
st(s) = stitch(es)
tr = triple
yo = yarn over hook

With larger hook ch6, join with a sl st into first ch to form a ring.

Round 1: (Work over starting tail of yarn), ch5 (counts as 1dc, ch2), (3dc into ring, 2ch) 3 times, 2dc into ring, join with a sl st into 3rd of 5ch. Gently pull on starting tail to tighten center of square.

Round 2: Sl st into 2ch sp, ch5, 2dc into same sp, *1rtrf into next dc, 1dc into next dc, 1rtrf into next dc, (2dc, ch2, 2dc) into next 2ch sp, rep from * twice more, 1rtrf into next dc, 1dc into next dc, 1rtrf into next dc, 1dc into first ch sp, join with a sl st into 3rd of 5ch. 7 sts on each side.

Round 3: Sl st into 2ch sp, ch5, 2dc into same sp, *(1rtrf into next dc, 1dc into next dc) 3 times, 1rtrf into next dc, (2dc, ch2, 2dc) into next 2ch sp, rep from * twice more, (1rtrf into next dc, 1dc into next dc) 3 times, 1rtrf into next dc, 1dc into first ch sp, join with a sl st into 3rd of 5ch. 11 sts on each side.

Round 4: Sl st into 2ch sp, ch5, 2dc into same sp, *(1rtrf into next dc, 1dc into next dc) 5 times, 1rtrf into next dc, (2dc, ch2, 2dc) into next 2ch sp, rep from * twice more, (1rtrf into next dc, 1dc into next dc) 5 times, 1rtrf into next dc, 1dc into first ch sp, join with a sl st into 3rd of 5ch. 15 sts on each side.

Round 5: Sl st into 2ch sp, ch5, 2dc into same sp, *(1rtrf into next dc, 1dc into next dc) 7 times, 1rtrf into next dc, (2dc, ch2, 2dc) into next 2ch sp, rep from * twice more, (1rtrf into next dc, 1dc into next dc) 7 times, 1rtrf into next dc, 1dc into first ch sp, join with a sl st into 3rd of 5ch. 19 sts on each side.

Round 7: Sl st into 2ch sp, ch3 (counts as first dc), (1dc into each of next 23 sts, 1dc into 2ch sp) 3 times, 1dc into each of next 23 sts, join with a sl st into 3rd of 3ch. 96 sts.

Round 8: ch3, skip st at base of ch, 1dc into each dc, join with a sl st into 3rd of 3ch. Rep last round 11 more times.

Border:

Change to smaller hook.

Next round: ch2, skip st at base of ch, *1rdcf in next dc, rdcb2tog over next 2dc, (1rdcf in next dc, 1rdcb in foll dc) 6 times, 1rdcf in next dc, rdcb2tog over next 2dc, (1rdcf in next dc, 1rdcb in foll dc) 7 times, rep from * twice more, ending last rep (1rdcf, 1rdcb) 6 times, 1rdcf in last dc, join with a sl st into 2nd of 2ch. 90 sts.

Next round: ch2, *1rdcf in next rdcf, 1rdcb in next rdcb, rep from * all around (treating rdcb2tog as 1rdcb), ending 1rdcf in rdcf, join with a sl st into 2nd of 2ch. Rep last round 3 more times. Fasten off.

Round 6: Sl st into 2ch sp, ch5, 2dc into same sp, *(1rtrf into next dc, 1dc into next dc) 9 times, 1rtrf into next dc, (2dc, ch2, 2dc) into next 2ch sp, rep from * twice more, (1rtrf into next dc, 1dc into next dc) 9 times, 1rtrf into next dc, 1dc into first ch sp, join with a sl st into 3rd of 5ch. 23 sts on each side.

Striped place mats

Simple to make, these stylish mats will color-coordinate your dining table.

These matching mats and coasters make stylish dining accessories. Worked in an easy stitch pattern, the textured stripes are enhanced by the dramatic color contrast of black, white, and fuchsia .

GETTING STARTED

⭐ *Simple stitch and stripe pattern with no shaping involved.*

Size:
Placemat: 13¾ x 10 inches (35 x 25cm)
Coaster: 5½ x 5½ inches (14 x 14cm)

How much yarn:
For 4 table settings:
2 x 100g (3½oz) balls of King Cole Bamboo Cotton in each of two colors: A—Black (shade 534) and B—White (shade 530)
1 ball of color C—Fuchsia (shade 536)

Hook:
4.00mm (G/6) crochet hook

Gauge:
18 sts and 13 rows measure 4 inches (10cm) square over patt on 4.00mm (G/6) hook
IT IS ESSENTIAL TO WORK TO THE STATED GAUGE TO ACHIEVE SUCCESS.

What you have to do:
Work foundation chain. Work pattern as instructed, changing color every two rows. Carry color not in use up side of work. Finish edges with border of single crochet.

The Yarn
King Cole Bamboo Cotton (approx. 230m/251 yards per 100g/3½oz ball) is 50% bamboo and 50% cotton in a double knitting weight yarn, which can be machine washed.

Instructions

Abbreviations:

ch = chain(s)
cm = centimeter(s)
cont = continue
dc = double crochet
foll = follows
hdc = half double crochet
mm = millimeter(s)
patt = pattern
rep = repeat
RS = right side
sc = single crochet
sl st = slip stitch
st(s) = stitch(es)

PLACE MAT:

With A, ch46. Cont in alternate stripes of 2 rows A and 2 rows B, carrying yarn not in use up side of work.

Foundation row: (RS) With A, work 1sc into 2nd ch from hook, *1hdc into next ch, 1dc into next ch, 1hdc into next ch, 1sc into next ch, rep from * to end, turn.

Row 1: With A, ch1, 1sc into first sc, *1hdc into next hdc, 1dc into next dc, 1hdc into next hdc, 1sc into next sc, rep from * to end, turn (omitting turning ch).

Row 2: With B, ch3 (counts as first dc), skip first sc, *1hdc into next dc, 1sc into next hdc, 1dc into next

sc, rep from * to end, turn (omitting turning ch).

Row 3: With B, ch3, skip first dc, *1hdc into next hdc, 1sc into next sc, 1hdc into next hdc, 1dc into next dc, rep from * to end, working last dc into 3rd of 3ch, turn.

Row 4: With A, ch1, 1sc into first dc, *1hdc into next hdc, 1dc into next sc, 1hdc into next hdc, 1sc into next dc, rep from * to end, working last sc into 3rd of 3ch, turn.

Rep Rows 1–4 8 more times, then work Row 1 again.

Cont in patt as set, work 8 more rows in stripes as foll: 2 rows C, 2 rows B, 2 rows

C, and 2 rows A. Do not fasten off, but turn and cont as foll:

Edging:

With A, ch1, work 1sc into each st to last (corner) st on this side, 2sc into corner st, cont in sc around rem 3 sides (working approximately 5sc into every 4 row ends) and 2sc into each corner st, ending 1sc into same place as first sc. Join with a sl st into first ch. Fasten off.

COASTER:

With A, ch26. Work Foundation row and cont in patt as given for Place mat, working 18 rows in stripes as foll: 2 rows A, 2 rows B, 2 rows A, 2 rows C, 2 rows B, 2 rows C, 2 rows A, 2 rows B, and 2 rows A. Fasten off.

Edging:

Work as given for Place mat.

Slouch socks

Perfect for keeping your toes cozy, these chunky socks
have bright striped tops.

With contrast-colored heel and toe and striped tops, these fun socks, worked in single crochet and an elongated stitch pattern, are bound to cheer you up.

GETTING STARTED

Stitches are straightforward, but there is a lot of shaping to concentrate on.

Size:

To fit women's shoe size: 6½–7½[7½–8½:8½–9½]

Foot length: 8½[9½:10¼] inches (22[24:26]cm)

Note: *Figures in brackets [ ] refer to larger sizes; where there is only one set of figures, it applies to all sizes.*

How much yarn:

2[2:3] x 50g (1¾oz) balls of Debbie Bliss Baby Cashmerino in main color A—Cream (shade 101)

1 ball in each 3 contrast colors: B—Pink (shade 029); C—Lilac (shade 033), and D—Turquoise (shade 031)

Hooks:

3.50mm (E/4) crochet hook

4.00mm (G/6) crochet hook

Gauge:

21 elongated sc and 18 rows measure 4 inches (10cm) square on 3.50mm (E/4) hook

IT IS ESSENTIAL TO WORK TO THE STATED GAUGE TO ACHIEVE SUCCESS.

What you have to do:

Work toe and heel in single crochet and foot in elongated sc in colors and shaping as instructed as directed. Work leg section in stripes and cluster pattern as directed. Work mainly in rounds (so no harsh seams or finishing required).

The Yarn

Debbie Bliss Baby Cashmerino (approx. 125m/136 yards per 50g/1¾oz ball) contains 50% merino wool, 33% microfiber, and 12% cashmere. It produces a soft, luxurious fabric that can be machine washed at a low temperature. There is an extensive palette of colors.

Instructions

Abbreviations:

alt = alternate
beg = beginning
ch = chain(s)
cm = centimeter(s)
cont = continue
dc = double crochet
elongated sc = insert hook into next st and draw a loop through, yo and draw through first loop on hook, yo and draw through both loops on hook
foll = follow(s)(ing)
hdc = half double crochet
inc = increase(ing)
mm = millimeter(s)
patt = pattern
rep = repeat
sc = single crochet
sl st = slip stitch
sp(s) = space(s)
st(s) = stitch(es)
yo = yarn over hook

SOCKS: (make 2)

With larger hook and B, ch9[9:11] for toe.

Round 1: Working into top loop only, work 1sc into 2nd ch from hook, 1sc into each of next 7[7:9]ch, now work 1sc into each loop along other side of ch. 18[18:22]sc.

Round 2: 1sc into first sc and mark this sc, work 2sc into next sc, (1sc inc), 1sc into each of next 6[6:8]sc, inc in next sc, 1sc into next sc and mark this sc, inc in next sc, 1sc into each of next 6[6:8] sc, inc in next sc (sc before marked sc). 22[22:26]sc.

Moving markers up on each round, work as foll:

Round 3: 1sc into each sc all around.

Round 4: 1sc into first marked sc, inc in next sc, 1sc into each sc to within 1sc of next marked sc, inc in next sc, 1sc into marked sc, inc in next sc, 1sc into each sc to within 1sc of first marked sc, inc in next sc. 26[26:30]sc.

Cont to inc 4 sc in this way (1sc each side

of marked sc) on every alt round until there are 34[38:46]sc, ending with a Round 3.

Remove second marker. Remaining marker indicates beg of rounds.

Cut off B and join in A. Change to smaller hook. Work foot as foll:

Patt round: 1 elongated sc into each sc all around. Rep last round until Sock measures 5½[6¼:7] inches (14[16:18]cm). (Length can be adjusted here and should be 3 inches (8cm) less than desired foot length, measured from back of heel to tip of toe.)

Place a marker on 18th[20th:24th]sc. Markers indicate sides of foot. Cont in elongated sc, working gusset by inc 1 st at each side of marked sts on next and every foll alt round until there are 54[58:66]sc. Remove markers.

Next row: Patt 12[13:15], do not turn but cut off A and join in C.

Now work heel in sc as foll:

Change to larger hook.

Row 1: With C, work 2sc into next st, 1sc into next st, 2sc into next st, sl st into next st, turn. 5sc.

Row 2: ch1, 1sc into first sc, (inc in next sc, 1sc into next sc) twice, sl st into next st of foot, turn. 7sc.

Row 3: ch1, 1sc into each of next 2sc, inc in next sc, 1sc into next sc, inc in next sc, 1sc into each of next 2sc, sl st into next st of foot, turn. 9sc.

Row 4: ch1, 1sc into each of next 3sc, inc in next sc, 1sc into next sc, inc in next sc, 1sc into each of next 3sc, sl st into next st of foot, turn. 11sc.

Row 5: ch1, 1sc into each of next 4sc, inc

in next sc, 1sc into next sc, inc in next sc, 1sc into each of next 4sc, sl st into next st of foot, turn. 13sc.

Row 6: ch1, 1sc into each of next 5sc, inc in next sc, 1sc into next sc, inc in next sc, 1sc into each of next 5sc, sl st into next st of foot, turn. 15sc.

3rd size only:

Row 7: ch1, 1sc into each of next 6sc, inc in next sc, 1sc into next sc, inc in next sc, 1sc into each of next 6sc, sl st into next st of foot, turn. 17sc.

All sizes:

Next row: ch1, 1sc into each of next 15[15:17]sc, sl st into next st of foot, turn.

Rep last row, working and joining heel to foot, until 12[13:15] rows and sts have been joined at each side of heel, turn. Cut off C and join in A.

Round 1: ch3 (counts as 1hdc and ch1), skip first sc, 1hdc into next sc, (ch1, skip next sc, 1hdc into next sc) 6[6:7] times, ch1, skip next sc, 1hdc into same st on foot as sl st, (ch1, skip next st, 1hdc into next st) 13[14:16] times, ch1, hdc into same st on foot as sl st, ch1, join with a sl st into first sp. 23[24:27] sps.

Cut off A and join in D.

Round 2: ch3 (counts as first dc), leaving last loop of each on hook work 2dc into first sp, yo and draw through all 3 loops on hook, *ch1, leaving last loop of each on hook work 3dc all into next sp, yo and draw through all 4 loops on hook (cluster formed), rep from * to end, finishing with ch1, join with a sl st into top of first cluster.

Round 3: ch3 (counts as 1hdc and ch1), 1hdc into into first sp, *ch1, 1hdc into next sp, rep from * to end, finishing with ch1, join with a sl st into first sp.

Round 4: ch3, leaving last loop of each on hook work 2dc into first sp, yo and draw through all 3 loops on hook, *ch1, work a cluster into next sp, rep from * to end, finishing with ch1, join with a sl st into top of first cluster.

The last 2 rounds form patt. Joining in and cutting off colors as required, cont in patt in stripes as foll: 1 round A, 3 rounds B, 1 round A, 3 rounds C, 1 round A, 3 rounds D, 1 round A, and 3 rounds B. Fasten off.

Sew in ends neatly.

Ruffle scarf

Lacy ruffles are used to create a scarf that has a nostalgic look.

This long lacy scarf, worked in a lightweight yarn, falls in frivolous ruffles, creating a flattering effect while also keeping your neck warm.

The Yarn

Sublime Extra Fine Merino Wool 4 Ply (approx. 175m/191 yards per 50g/1¾oz ball) contains 100% merino wool. Spun from the finest-quality fibers, this luxurious yarn can be machine washed at a low temperature. There is a small range of colors to choose from.

GETTING STARTED

★ ★ *Pattern is straightforward, but working rows along length of scarf needs patience.*

Size:
Finished scarf is approximately 73 inches (185cm) long when hanging x 4 inches (10cm) wide when flat

How much yarn:
4 x 50g (1¾oz) balls of Sublime Extra Fine Merino Wool 4 Ply in Glamour (shade 130)

Hook:
4.00mm (G/6) crochet hook

Gauge:
1 patt rep measures approximately 2 inches (5cm) across at outer edge and frill measures approximately 4 inches (10cm) wide on 4.00mm (G/6) hook
IT IS ESSENTIAL TO WORK TO THE STATED GAUGE TO ACHIEVE SUCCESS.

What you have to do:
Make an extra-long foundation chain (to equal length of scarf). Work foundation row in single crochet. Work first side of frill in a lacy pattern, doubling number of stitches on first row to create a ruffle effect. Make picot edging with chain loops along outer edge. Work second side of frill in same way by working into stitches on other side of foundation chain.

Instructions

Abbreviations:

ch = chain(s)

cm = centimeter(s)

dc = double crochet

dc2tog = work 1dc in each of next 2 dc leaving last loop of each on hook, yo and draw through all 3 loops

patt = pattern

rem = remain

rep = repeat

sc = single crochet

sl st = slip stitch

sp(s) = space(s)

st(s) = stitch(es)

tr = treble(s)

yo = yarn over hook

Ch332.

Foundation row: 1sc into 2nd ch from hook, 1sc into each ch to end, turn. 331 sts.

Row 1: ch5 (counts as first tr and ch1), 1tr into next st, *ch1, 1tr into next st, rep from * to end, turn. 331 sts and 330 ch sps.

Row 2: ch1, 1sc into first st, ch2, skip next ch sp and st (i.e. 2 sts), 1sc into next ch sp or st, *skip next 2 sts, 6dc into next st or ch sp, skip 2 sts, 1sc into next ch sp or st, ch2, skip 2 sts, 1sc into next st or ch sp, rep from * to end, turn.

Row 3: ch1, 1sc into first sc, ch2, *1dc into next dc, (ch1, 1dc into next dc) 5 times, 1sc into next 2ch sp, rep from * to last 2sc omitting 1sc at end of last rep, ch2, 1sc into last sc, turn.

Row 4: ch3 (counts as first dc), (1dc into next dc, ch2) 5 times, *dc2tog, ch2, (1dc into next dc, ch2) 4 times, rep from * to last dc, work 1dc into next dc until 2 loops rem on hook, 1dc into last sc until 3 loops rem on hook, yo and draw through all 3 loops, turn.

Row 5: ch1, 1sc into first st, 3sc into first ch2 sp, *ch7, 3sc into next 2ch sp, rep from * to last 2dc, 1sc into 3rd

of 3ch, do not fasten off but sl st along row ends of ruffle to foundation ch, do not turn.

Row 6: Work as given for Row I but working into other side of sts in foundation ch, turn.

Rows 7–10: Work as given for Rows 2–5. Fasten off.

Chevron pillow

Here's a great example of how a traditional pattern can be given a modern twist by choosing adventurous colors.

Work chevrons in varying widths and a selection of funky colors for this contemporary pillow. The back is worked in plain double crochet, and has a buttoned opening.

The Yarn

Debbie Bliss Rialto DK (approx. 105m/ 114 yards per 50g/1¾oz ball) contains 100% extra-fine merino wool. It produces a soft, luxurious fabric, machine-washable at a low temperature. There is a fabulous color range for contemporary work.

GETTING STARTED

⭐⭐ *Chevron pattern is easy to follow, but there are a lot of color changes.*

Size:
12 x 12 inches (30 x 30cm)

How much yarn:
1 x 50g (1¾oz) ball of Debbie Bliss Rialto DK in each of five colors: A—Red (shade 12); B—Turquoise (shade 24); C—Orange (shade 32); D—Lime (shade 09) and E—Teal (shade 20)
2 balls in color F—Bright Pink (shade 34)

Hooks:
3.50mm (E/4) crochet hook
4.00mm (G/6) crochet hook

Additional items:
2 x 1⅜-inch (3.5cm) buttons
12 x 12-inch (30 x 30cm) pillow form
13 x 25-inch (33 x 63cm) rectangle of cotton lining fabric in a toning color

Matching sewing thread and needle

Gauge:
1 patt rep (11 sts) measures 2½ inches (6.5cm) and 11 rows measure 5 inches (13cm) over patt on 3.50mm (E/4) hook
IT IS ESSENTIAL TO WORK TO THE STATED GAUGE TO ACHIEVE SUCCESS.

What you have to do:
Work pillow front in chevron pattern and stripes. When working stripes, always change to new color on last part of stitch in old color. Work pillow backs in double crochet throughout and one color, with borders in single crochet and a contrast color. Make buttonholes in back border. Sew simple fabric cover for pillow form so that it does not show through chevron pattern.

Instructions

Abbreviations:

ch = chain(s)

cm = centimeter(s)

cont = continue

dc = double crochet

dc2tog = work 1dc into each of next 2 sts leaving last loop of each of hook, yarn round hook and draw through all 3 loops

foll = follows

hdc = half double crochet

patt = pattern

rep = repeat

RS = right side

sc = single crochet

sl st = slip stitch

st(s) = stitch(es)

tog = together

tr = triple(s)

WS = wrong side

yo = yarn over hook

FRONT:

With larger hook and A, Ch57. Change to smaller hook.

Foundation row: (RS) 1dc into 4th ch from hook, 1dc into each of next ch3, *3dc into next ch, 1dc into each of next ch4, skip next ch2, 1dc into each of next ch4, rep from * 3 more times, 3dc into next ch, 1dc into each of last ch5, turn.

Row 1: ch3 (counts as first dc), skip st at base of ch and foll st, 1dc into each of next 4 sts, *3dc into next st, 1dc into each of next 4 sts, skip next 2 sts, 1dc into each of next 4 sts, rep from * 3 more times, 3dc into next st, 1dc into each of next 4 sts, skip next st, 1dc into 3rd of 3ch, turn. The last row forms patt. Cont in patt, working in stripe sequence as foll and always joining in new color on last part of last st in old color:

3 more rows A; 2 rows B; 3 rows C; 1 row B; 2 rows D; 3 rows F; 2 rows C; 1 row E; 2 rows D; and 4 rows A.

Next row: With F, ch3 (counts as first dc), skip st at base of ch, *dc2tog into next 2 sts, 1hdc into next st, 1sc into next st, sl st into each of next 3 sts, 1sc into next st, 1hdc into next st, dc2tog into next 2 sts, 1tr into sp between sts, rep from * 3 more times, dc2tog into next 2 sts, 1hdc into next st, 1sc into next, sl st into each of next 3 sts, 1sc into next st, 1hdc into next st, dc2tog into next 2 sts, 1dc into 3rd of 3ch, turn.

Next row: ch1 (does not count as a st), 1sc into each st to end, working last sc into 3rd of 3ch. Fasten off.

Turn Front around and work along other side of foundation ch as foll:

With RS facing, join F to first st, ch1, 1sc into first st, 1hdc into each of next 2 sts, dc2tog into next 2sts, *1dc into next st, dc2tog into next 2 sts, 1hdc into each of next 2 sts, 1sc into first of 2ch, 1sc into sp, 1sc into 2nd of 2ch, 1hdc into each of next 2 sts, dc2tog into next 2 sts, rep from * 3 more times, 1dc into next st,

dc2tog into next 2 sts, 1hdc into each of next 2 sts, 1sc into last st, turn.
Next row: ch1 (does not count as a st), 1sc into each st to end. Fasten off.

LOWER BACK:
With larger hook and F, 52ch. Change to smaller hook.
Foundation row: 1dc into 4th ch from hook, 1dc into each ch to end, turn. 50 sts.
Row 1: ch3 (counts as first dc), skip st at base of ch, 1dc into each st to end, working last dc into 3rd of 3ch, turn. Work 11 more rows in dc.

Border:
Change to B.
Next row: ch1 (does not count as a st), 1sc into each st to end, working last sc into 3rd of 3ch, turn. Work 3 more rows in sc.
Buttonhole row 1: ch1, 1sc into each of next 16 sts, ch3, skip next 4 sts, 1sc into each of next 10 sts, ch3, skip next 4 sts, 1sc into each of next 16 sts, turn.
Buttonhole row 2: Work in sc, working 4sc into each 3ch space, turn.
Work 2 more rows in sc. Fasten off.

TOP BACK:
Work as given for Lower Back, working 8 rows in sc for border and omitting buttonholes.

 # Finishing

Block pillow pieces to shape, lightly spray with clean water, and leave until completely dry. Place front WS down on a flat surface and lay lower back on top of it, RS down and with buttonhole border in center. Now lay top back in place, RS down and overlapping borders in center. Join with a backstitch seam around outer edges. Turn RS out and sew on buttons to match buttonholes.

Pillow lining:
Fold lining fabric in half with RS facing. Taking ⅝-inch (1.5cm) seam allowances, sew along two adjacent sides, leaving one side open. Turn RS out and press seam allowances along open side to WS. Insert pillow form and neatly slipstitch seam closed.
Insert covered pillow form into cover and fasten buttons.

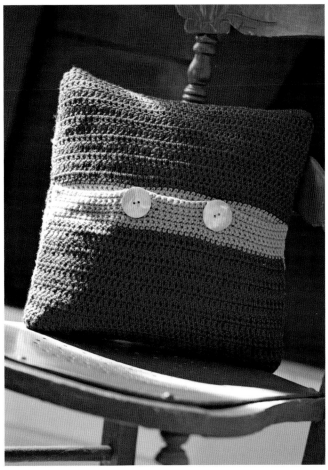

Versatile mitts

Keep your fingers covered up or free—the choice
is yours with these mitts.

Worked in a subtle felted tweed yarn and ridged single crochet pattern, these fingerless mitts have a button-down top for extra warmth when you need it.

GETTING STARTED

★★ *Easy stitch pattern but lots of details, and shaping requires concentration.*

Size:
To fit an average-sized woman's hand

How much yarn:
2 x 50g (1¾oz) balls of Rowan Felted Tweed DK in Watery (shade 152)

Hook:
3.50mm (E/4) crochet hook

Additional items:
2 small buttons

Gauge:
22 sts and 20 rows measure 4 inches (10cm) square over patt on 3.50mm (E/4) hook
IT IS ESSENTIAL TO WORK TO THE STATED GAUGE TO ACHIEVE SUCCESS.

What you have to do:
Work wristband first in mock rib pattern. Pick up stitches for mitt along side edge of wristband and continue in ridged single crochet pattern. Shape for thumb and finger section as directed.

The Yarn
Rowan Felted Tweed DK (approx. 175m/191 yards per 50g/1¾oz ball) contains 50% merino wool, 25% alpaca and 25% viscose. Machine-washable, it makes a soft, matted fabric. It comes in a range of tweed shades.

 # Instructions

LEFT MITT:
Wristband:
Ch16.

Foundation row: (RS) 1sc in 2nd ch from hook, 1sc in each ch to end, turn. 16 sts (counting first ch as 1 st).

Row 1: ch1, skip st at base of ch, 1scb in each st, ending 1sc in ch1, turn.

Rep last row 34 more times, ending with a WS row. 36 rows in all. Fasten off.

Main part:
Round 1: With RS of wristband facing, rejoin yarn at right of one long edge, ch1, skip first row, 1sc in side of each of next 35 rows, join into a circle with a sl st in first ch. 36 sts.

Patt round: ch1 (counts as first sc), skip st at base of ch, 1scb in each st to end, join with a sl st in first ch.

Shape for thumb:
Round 3: ch1, skip st at base of ch, 1scb in each of next 16scb, (2scb in next scb) twice, 1scb in each of next 17scb, join with a sl st in first ch. 38 sts.

Round 4: As Patt round.

Round 5: ch1, skip st at base of ch, 1dcb in each of next 16scb, 2scb in next scb, 1scb in each of next 2scb, 2scb in

Abbreviations:

alt = alternate
beg = beginning
ch = chain
cm = centimeter(s)
cont = continue
dec = decrease(s)
inc = increas(es)(ing)
mm = millimeter(s)
patt = pattern
rep = repeat
RS = right side
sc = single crochet
scb = double crochet
working into back
loop only
scb2tog = (insert hook
in back loop only of next
st, yo and draw a loop
through) twice, yo and
draw through all 3 loops
sp = space
sl st = slip stitch
st(s) = stitch(es)
tog = together
WS = wrong side
yo = yarn over hook

next scb, 1scb in each of next 17scb, join with a sl st in first ch. 40 sts.

Round 6: As Patt round.

Cont in this way, inc 2 sts (with 2 extra scb between incs) on next and every alt round, for another 8 rounds. 48 sts; 14 rounds from wristband.

Shape thumb hole:

Round 15: ch1, skip st at base of ch, 1scb in each of next 17scb, ch2, skip next 12scb, 1scb in each of next 18scb, join with a sl st in first ch.

Round 16: ch1, skip st at base of ch, 1scb in each of next 17scb, 1sc in each of 2ch, 1scb in each of next 18scb, join with a sl st in first ch. 38 sts.

Rounds 17–22: Patt 6 rounds.

Separate fingers:

(**Note:** next 2 rounds are worked in plain sc not scb.)

Separating round: ch1, skip st at base of ch, 1sc in each of next 3scb, ch3, 1sl st in last sc (picot made), 1sc in each of next 4scb, 1 picot, 1sc in each of next 5scb, 1 picot, 1sc in each of next 12scb, 1sc in tip of last picot made, 1sc in each of next 5scb, 1sc in tip of second picot made, 1sc in each of next 4scb, 1sc in tip of first picot made, 1sc in each of next 4scb, join with a sl st in first ch.

Last round: ch1, skip st at base of ch, 1sc in each of next 3sc, 1sc in right leg of picot, ch1, 1sc in left leg of picot (1ch sp made), 1sc in each of next 4sc, 1ch sp over next picot, 1sc in each of next 5sc, 1ch sp over next picot, 1sc in each of next 12sc, 1sc in 3rd 1ch sp made, skip sc in tip of picot, 1sc in each of next 5sc, 1sc in 2nd 1ch sp made, skip sc in tip of picot, 1sc in each of next 4sc, 1sc in first 1ch sp made, skip sc in tip of picot, 1sc in each of next 4sc, join with a sl st in first ch.

Fasten off.

Border for finger section:

Ch6. Work Foundation row as given for Wristband (6 sts), then work 5 rows as given for Row 1 of wristband.

Row 7: ch6, 1sc in 2nd ch from hook, 1sc in each of next 4ch, patt to end, turn. 12 sts.

Rows 8 and 9: Work 2 rows in patt.

Row 10: ch1, skip first scb, 1scb in each of next 5scb, ch3, skip next 3 sts, 1scb in each of next 2scb, 1sc in ch1, turn.

Row 11: ch1, skip first scb, 1scb in each of next 2scb, 1scb in same place as last st tog with 1sc in 3ch sp, 1sc in 3ch sp, 1sc in ch3 sp tog with 1scb in next scb, 1scb in same place as last insertion, patt to end, turn. 12 sts.

Rows 12 and 13: Patt to end.

Row 14: ch1, skip st at base of ch, 1scb in each of next 5scb, turn. 6 sts.

Work 5 rows in patt, ending with a RS row. 19 rows in all. Fasten off. *

Finger section:

Rejoin yarn to joining st at beg of last round in scb (Round 22), below finger separating rounds and work across palm, ch1, (1scb in same place as next st of separating round) 18 times, then with RS of flap border facing, work 1sc in side edge of each of 19 rows of unshaped side edge, join with a sl st in first ch. 38 sts.

** Work 10 rounds in patt.

Dec round 1: ch1, skip st at base of ch, scb2tog over next 2 sts, 1scb in each of next 13 sts, scb2tog over next 2 sts, 1scb in each of next 2 sts, scb2tog over next 2 sts, 1sc in each of next 13 sts, scb2tog over next 2 sts, 1scb in next st, join with a sl st in first ch. 34 sts.

Dec round 2: ch1, skip st at base of ch, scb2tog over next 2 sts, 1scb in each of next 11 sts, scb2tog over next 2 sts, 1scb in each of next 2 sts, scb2tog over next 2 sts, 1sc in each of next 11 sts, scb2tog over next 2 sts, 1scb in next st, join with a sl st in first ch. 30 sts.

Work 3 more dec rounds in same way, working 2 sts less between first and 2nd decs and 3rd and 4th decs, on each round. 18 sts. Fasten off.

Thumb:

With RS of work facing, rejoin yarn at base of first of 2ch made on round15.

Round 1: ch1, skip st at base of ch, 1scb in each of next 12scb, 1sc in 2nd of 2ch, join with a sl st in first ch. 14 sts. Work 10 rounds in patt.

Dec round: ch1, skip st at base of ch, (scb2tog) 6 times, 1scb in last scb, join with a sl st in first ch. Fasten off.

RIGHT MITT:

Work as given for Left Mitt to *.

Finger section:

With RS of flap border facing, rejoin yarn at right of long unshaped side edge, ch1, skip first row, 1sc in side edge of each of next 18 rows, with palm of right mitt facing, 1scb in each of last 19 sts of last round in scb (round 22), join with a sl st in first ch. 38 sts.

Complete as given for Left Mitt from ** to end.

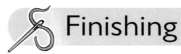 # Finishing

Join seam at top of finger section. Sew down short edges of finger section border to straight lines of sts at each side of mitt. Gather top of thumb tightly and secure. Join wristband seam. Sew on button to match buttonhole.

Spiral table mat

Create this stunning centerpiece for your table by crocheting with strips of fabric.

This fabulous table center is worked in continuous rounds of single crochet from strips of fabric. A core of unbleached muslin gives the mat bulk and stability.

The Yarn

This design is based on a rag-rug technique and uses strips of fabric instead of yarn. The fabrics can be any old cotton materials (patterned and solid-coloured) and should be washed then cut into strips as described on page 55.

GETTING STARTED

★ ★ *Easy stitches, but working with strips of fabric requires practice.*

Size:
20 inches (50cm) in diameter

How much yarn:
1 yard (1 meter) of unbleached muslin or old sheeting for the core
Selection of old washed cotton fabrics, including dress materials and shirting

Hook:
8.00mm (L/11) crochet hook

Additional items:
Needle and sewing thread
Short piece of yarn

Gauge:
First 6 rounds measure 6 inches (15cm) in diameter on 8.00mm (L/11) hook

What you have to do:
Cut up fabrics as directed. Work throughout over strip of core fabric for bulk. Work in continuous rounds of single crochet. Join in new fabrics as required.

Notes:

• You can prepare the fabric first and roll it up into small balls, or cut each piece as you go. Cut a strip approximately ¾ inch (2cm) wide from one edge of the piece and stop cutting when you are ¾ inch (2cm) from the far end. Now turn the fabric and start cutting another ¾ inch (2cm) down, so that you have one long strip. Continue in this way until the end of the piece of fabric.

• Change colors as you wish during the work. When you need to join in a new length, fold 1½ inches (4cm) at one end inside the short end of the working length and work one or more stitches with a double thickness to secure the new length.

• For the core, you will need a 2-inch (5-cm) wide strip of unbleached muslin or old sheeting.

![instructions icon] # Instructions

Abbreviations:
beg = beginning
cm = centimeter(s)
mm = millimeter(s)
sc = single crochet
st = stitch

TABLE MAT:

Twist first 2½ inches (6cm) of core fabric into a loop and sew short end down to secure. Hold loop so that long end lies toward left.

Round 1: Fasten on one end of a fabric strip and work 10sc into loop. Do not join into a round, but continue working in a continuous spiral.

Round 2: Working each st over core fabric throughout, work 2sc into each st to end. 20sc. Tie a length of yarn to next st to act as a marker for beg of next and subsequent rounds.

Round 3: (1sc into next sc, 2sc into next sc) to end. 30sc.

Round 4: 1sc into each sc to end.

Round 5: (1sc into each of next 2sc, 2sc into next sc) to end. 40sc.

Round 6: 1sc into each sc to end.

Round 7: (1sc into each of next 3sc, 2sc into next sc) to end. 50sc.

Round 8: (1sc into each of next 4sc, 2sc into next sc) to end. 60sc.

Round 9: (1sc into each of next 5sc, 2sc into next sc) to end. 70sc.

Rounds 10 and 11: 1sc into each sc to end.

Round 12: As Round 8. 84sc.

Round 13: As Round 9. 98sc.

Round 14: 1sc into each sc to end.

Round 15: (1sc into each of next 6sc, 2sc into next sc) to end. 112sc.

Round 16: 1sc into each sc to end.

Round 17: (1sc into each of next 7sc, 2sc into next sc) to end. 126sc.

Round 18: 1sc into each sc to end.

Round 19: (1sc into each of next 8sc, 2sc into next sc) to end. 140sc.

20th and 21st rounds: 1sc into each sc to end.

Fasten off and sew loose end to back of work.

HOW TO
TO CUT THE FABRIC

Old cotton fabric, either solid-colored or patterned, is perfect for this technique. Cut it into strips, roll it into balls, and you're ready to start crocheting this stunning table centerpiece.

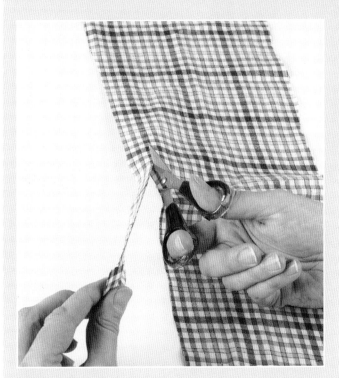

1 Select a mixture of cotton fabrics with a similar color palette. They can be be solid-coloured or patterned, such as stripes or plaid. Wash the fabric first, then cut it into strips about ¾ inch (2cm) wide.

2 To make a continuous strip, stop cutting ¾ inch (2cm) from the end of the piece and turn the fabric. Continue cutting in the opposite direction and repeat this each time you reach the edge of the fabric.

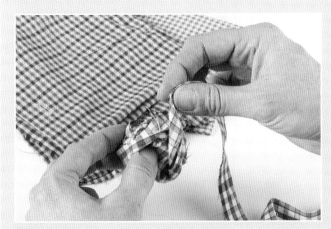

3 This will give you a long continuous strip of fabric that is ¾ inch (2cm) wide. Wind each strip up into a small ball. Repeat this with each type of fabric, then you are ready to start work. Change colors as you wish, swapping from ball to ball.

Cobweb wrap

Mohair and silk combine to make the light and luxurious yarn for this stole.

Light and fluffy as a feather and lacy as a cobweb, this wrap is worked in a gorgeous mohair yarn and openwork pattern.

GETTING STARTED

★★ *Straight strip of fabric, but lace mesh pattern requires concentration.*

Size:
Wrap measures approximately 18 x 61 inches (47 x 154cm)

How much yarn:
3 x 25g (1oz) balls of Debbie Bliss Angel in Blue/ Green (shade 09)

Hook:
4.50mm (size 7) crochet hook

Gauge:
1 rep of patt measures 4 inches (10cm) across x 4⅜ inches (11cm) deep on 4.50mm (UK 7) hook
IT IS ESSENTIAL TO WORK TO THE STATED GAUGE TO ACHIEVE SUCCESS.

What you have to do:
Work throughout in lace mesh pattern incorporating motifs as directed. Work narrow edging around wrap.

The Yarn
Debbie Bliss Angel (approx. 200m/218 yards per 100g/1oz ball) is a blend of 76% superkid mohair and 24% silk. It produces a luxurious silky soft handwash fabric. There is a wide range of colors.

Instructions

Abbreviations:

ch = chain(s)

cm = centimeter(s)

cont = continue

dc = double crochet

dtr2tog = yo 3 times, insert hook in specified st, *yo and draw a loop through, (yo and draw through first 2 loops on hook) 3 times * (2 loops left on hook), yo 3 times, insert hook in next specified st, rep from * to *, yo and draw through all 3 loops on hook

foll = follow(s)(ing)

mm = millimeter(s)

patt = pattern

rep = repeat

RS = right side

sc = single crochet

sl st = slip stitch

sp = spaces

st(s) = stitch(es)

dtr = double triple

yo = yarn over hook

WRAP:

Ch76.

Foundation row: (RS) 1dc into 6th ch from hook, (ch1, skip ch1, 1dc into next ch) 3 times, *ch4, skip ch1, dtr2tog working first part of st into next ch, then skip ch3 and work second part of st into next ch, ch4, skip ch1, 1dc into next ch, (ch1, skip ch1, 1dc into next ch) 4 times, rep from * to end, turn.

Cont in patt as foll:

Row 1: ch4 (counts as 1dc, ch1), skip first sp, 1dc into next dc, (ch1, skip ch1, 1dc into next dc) 3 times, *ch3, sl st into top of dtr2tog, ch3, 1dc into next dc, (ch1, skip ch1, 1dc into next dc) 4 times, rep from * to end, working last dc into 4th of 5ch (and 3rd of 4ch for subsequent rows), turn.

Row 2: ch4, skip first sp, 1dc into next dc,

(ch1, skip ch1, 1dc into next dc) 3 times, *ch4, sl st into sl st, ch4, 1dc into next dc, (ch1, skip ch1, 1dc into next dc) 4 times, rep from * to end, working last dc into 3rd of 4ch, turn.

Row 3: ch4, skip first sp, 1dc into next dc, (ch1, skip ch1, 1dc into next dc) 3 times, *ch1, (1dtr, ch3, 1dtr) into sl st, ch1, 1dc into next dc, (ch1, skip ch1, 1dc into next dc) 4 times, rep from * to end, working last dc into 3rd of 4ch, turn.

Row 4: ch7 (counts as 1dc, ch4), skip first sp, dtr2tog working first part of st into next dc, then skip next dc and work second part of st into foll dc, ch4, 1dc into next dc, *ch1, 1dc into next dtr, ch1, 1dc into 2nd of next ch3, ch1, 1dc into next dtr, ch1, 1dc into next dc, ch4, dtr2tog working first part of st into next dc, then skip next dc and work second part of st into foll dc, ch4, 1dc into next dc, rep from * to end, working last dc into 3rd of 4ch, turn.

Row 5: ch6 (counts as 1dc, ch3), sl st into top of dtr2tog, ch3, 1dc into next dc, *(ch1, skip ch1, 1dc into next dc) 4 times, ch3, sl st into top of dtr2tog, ch3, 1dc into next dc, rep from * to end, working last dc into 3rd of 7ch, turn.

Row 6: ch7 (counts as 1dc, ch4), sl st into sl st, ch4, 1dc into next dc, *(ch1, skip ch1, 1dc into next dc) 4 times, ch4, sl st into sl st, ch4, 1dc into next dc, rep from * to end, working last dc into 3rd of 6ch, turn.

Row 7: ch4 (counts as 1dc, ch1), (1dtr, ch3, 1dtr) into sl st, ch1, 1dc into next dc, *(ch1, skip ch1, 1dc into next dc) 4 times, ch1, (1dtr, ch3, 1dtr) into sl st, ch1, 1dc into next dc, rep from * to end, working last dc into 3rd of 7ch, turn.

Row 8: ch4 (counts as 1dc, ch1), 1dc into dtr, ch1, 1dc into 2nd of next ch3, ch1, 1dc into next tr, ch1, 1dc into next dc, *ch4, dtr2tog working first part of st into next dc, then skip next dc and work second part of st into foll dc, ch4, 1dc into next dc, ch1, 1dc into dtr, ch1, 1dc into 2nd of next ch3, ch1, 1dc into next dtr, ch1, 1dc into next dc, rep from * to end, working last dc into 3rd of 4ch, turn.

The last 8 rows form patt. Rep them 11 more times, then work Rows 1–3 again (wrap should measure 54 inches / 138cm). Turn at end of last row but do not fasten off.

Edging:

Round 1: 1sc into each st along top edge, 3sc into first row end, 2sc into each row-end down first side, 1sc into each ch along lower edge, 3sc into first row end, 1sc into each row end up second side, join with a sl st into first sc.

Round 2: ch3 (counts as first dc), 1dc into next sc, *(ch1, skip 1sc, 1dc into each of next 2sc) to next corner, ch3, 1dc into each of next 2sc, rep from * 3 more times omitting 2dc at end of last rep, join with a sl st into 3rd of 3ch. Fasten off.

Bobble hat

This close-fitting hat makes the most of the contrasting textures between the crochet and the furry pom pom.

Made in a flecked bulky yarn and textured pattern, this snug-fitting hat is trimmed with an eye-catching "furry" pom pom.

The Yarn

Sirdar Denim Ultra (approx. 75m/82 yards per 100g/3½oz ball) is a blend of 60% acrylic, 25% cotton, and 15% wool. The finished result resembles denim. There are plenty of denim-look colors to choose from and it can be machine washed. Sirdar Funky Fur (approx. 90m/98 yards per 50g/1¾oz ball) is 100% acrylic. It is a novelty yarn with an eyelash finish that resembles fur. There are bright shades, as well as neutral colors such as this to choose from.

GETTING STARTED

★★ *Quick to make, but working clusters and shaping can be a challenge.*

Size:

To fit an average adult woman's head

Hat measures 23 inches (58cm) in circumference x 7½ inches (19cm) deep

How much yarn:

1 x 100g (3½oz) ball of Sirdar Denim Ultra in color A—Starling (shade 507)

1 x 50g (1¾oz) ball of Sirdar Funky Fur in color B—Latte (shade 550)

Hooks:

4.00mm (G/6) crochet hook

5.00mm (H/8) crochet hook

Additional item:

Piece of cardboard or pom pom maker

Gauge:

12 sts measure 4¼ inches (11cm) and 8 rows measure 2½ inches (6.5cm) over patt using A on 5.00mm (H/8) hook

IT IS ESSENTIAL TO WORK TO THE STATED GAUGE TO ACHIEVE SUCCESS.

What you have to do:

Work main pattern in single crochet with clusters on alternating rows. Shape crown by decreasing on single crochet rows. Make pom pom in contrast-textured yarn.

Instructions

Abbreviations:

ch = chain
cm = centimeter(s)
cont = continue
foll = follows
mm = millimeter(s)
patt = pattern
rem = remaining
rep = repeat
sc2(3)tog = into each of next 2(3) sts work: (insert hook into st, yo and draw a loop through), yo and draw through all 3(4) loops
sc = single crochet
st(s) = stitch(es)
tog = together
WS = wrong side
yo = yarn over hook

HAT:

With smaller hook and A, ch65.

Foundation row: 1sc into 2nd ch from hook, 1sc into each ch to end, turn. 64 sts.

Next row: ch1 (does not count as a st), 1sc into each st to end, turn.

Change to larger hook.

Work 1 more row in sc as before.

Cont in patt as foll:

Row 1: (WS) ch1 (does not count as a st), *1sc into each of next 2 sts, work 1 cluster into next st as foll: (yo, insert hook into st and draw through a loop, yo and draw through first 2 loops on hook) twice, yo and draw through all 3 loops on hook, rep from * to last st, 1sc into last st, turn.

Row 2: ch1, 1sc into next st, *1sc into next cluster, 1sc into each of next 2 sts, rep from * to end, turn.

Row 3: ch1, 1sc into next st, *1 cluster into next st, 1sc into each of next 2 sts, rep from * to end, turn.

Row 4: ch1, *1sc into each of next 2 sts, 1sc into next cluster, rep from * to last st, 1sc into last st, turn.

These 4 rows form patt. Rep them once more, then work Row 1 again.

Shape crown:

Row 1: ch1, *(sc3tog) twice, 1sc into each of next 6 sts, rep from * to last 4 sts, sc3tog, 1sc into last st, turn. 42 sts.

Row 2: ch1, *1sc into each of next 2 sts, 1 cluster into next st, rep from * to end, turn.

Row 3: Work in sc.

Row 4: ch1, 1sc into next st, *1 cluster into next st, 1sc into each of next 2 sts, rep from * to last 2 sts, 1 cluster into next st, 1sc into next st, turn.

Row 5: ch1, *sc3tog, 1sc into each of next 6 sts, rep from * to last 6 sts, sc3tog, 1sc into each of next 3 sts, turn. 32 sts.

Row 6: ch1, *1sc into each of next 2 sts, 1 cluster into next st, rep from * to last 2 sts, 1sc into each of next 2 sts, turn.

Row 7: ch1, *sc3tog, 1sc into each of next 6 sts, rep from * to last 5 sts, sc3tog, 1sc into each of next 2 sts, turn. 24 sts.
Row 8: Work as given for Row 2 of crown shaping.
Row 9: *Sc3tog, rep from * to end. 8 sts.
Row 10: Work in sc.
Row 11: (Sc3tog) twice, dc2tog. 3 sts. Cut off yarn, leaving a long end for joining back seam. Thread yarn through rem sts and fasten off securely.

 ## Finishing

Join back seam with mattress (edge to edge) stitch. With B, make a pom pom 2 inches (5cm) in diameter. This can be done with a pom pom maker. Alternatively, cut 2 cardboard circles of 2-inches (5cm) diameter with holes of ¾ inch (2cm) diameter in the center. Thread several strands of yarn into a tapestry needle and hold the two rings together. Wind the yarn around the rings, taking it through the hole and then around the edge. Re-thread the needle as necessary until the hole is filled with yarn. Using sharp scissors, cut through the yarn, slipping the blade of the scissors between the two rings and cutting around the edge. Ease the rings apart and tie a length of yarn firmly around the strands in the middle of the rings. Leave the yarn end. Pull the rings apart and off the yarn at each end. Trim off any uneven strands and fluff the pom poms into perfect rounds. Thread the yarn end into the needle and sew the pom pom to the center of the crown.

Red-hot rug

Three shades of red are combined to make this retro-style rug.

The dense tweedy texture of this rug is enhanced by subtle shading, achieved by joining in the new yarn gradually along with the old one.

The Yarn

Debbie Bliss Luxury Tweed Chunky (approx. 100m/109 yards per 100g/3½oz ball) is a blend of 90% wool and 10% angora. Handwash only, it produces a luxurious and thick fabric with subtle slubs of color, which create a tweedy effect.

GETTING STARTED

★★ *Basic fabric with no shaping but care is needed with yarn color changes for the shaded effect.*

Size:
25 x 35½ inches (64 x 90cm)

How much yarn:
2 x 100g (3½oz) hanks of Debbie Bliss Luxury Tweed Chunky in each of 3 colors: A—Dark Red (shade 20); B—Bright Red (shade 07); C—Orange (shade 09)

Hook:
7.00mm (K/10½) crochet hook

Gauge:
10 sts and 8 rows measure 4 inches (10cm) square over hdc on 7.00mm (K/10½) hook
IT IS ESSENTIAL TO WORK TO THE STATED GAUGE TO ACHIEVE SUCCESS.

What you have to do:
Read instructions at start of rug to wind hanks into balls as specified. Read note on joining in new yarn—split two colors and work with both together for a while to achieve a subtle, random change of color. Work throughout in rows of half double crochet. Work edging around rug in rounds of single crochet.

Instructions

Abbreviations:

approx = approximately
beg = beginning
ch = chain
cm = centimeter(s)
cont = continue
foll = following
hdc = half double crochet
m = meters
mm = millimeter(s)
rep = repeat
RS = right side
sc = single crochet
sl st = slip stitch
sp = space
st(s) = stitch(es)
WS = wrong side

Note:

New yarn can be joined at beg or at any point in a row. When joining in new yarn, work until there is approx 7 yards (6.5 meters) of old ball of yarn left, carefully split the 2 strands and discard one of them. Mark out 7 yards (6.5 meters) at the start of new ball of yarn and split this in 2, also discarding one of them. Cont combining the 2 split lengths of old and new yarns. Do not worry if yarn breaks where it is split—simply knot ends together and keep working. Any knots will be hidden in the stitches or can be sewn in when the rug is complete.

RUG:

Before you start, wind 1 hank of each shade into large balls; wind remaining hank of each into 2 balls of equal weight. With large ball of A, ch62.

Foundation row: (RS) 1 hdc into 3rd ch from hook, 1 hdc into each ch to end, turn. 60 sts.

Row 1: ch2 (does not count as a st), 1 hdc into each hdc to end, omitting turning ch, turn.

Rep last row until there is approx 7 yards (6.5 meters) of yarn left. Foll instructions on joining yarn, join in and cont with large ball of B. Cont until there is approx 7 yards (6.5 meters) of yarn left and then join in and cont with large ball of C.

Cont until there is approx 7 yards (6.5 meters) of yarn left and then join in small ball of A. When there is approx 7 yards (6.5 meters) of yarn left, join in small ball of B; when there is approx 7 yards (6.5 meters) of yarn left, join in small ball of C; when there is approx 7 yards (6.5 meters) of yarn left, join in small ball of A. Cont in A until rug measures approx 34 inches (86cm) from beg, ending with a WS row.

Edging:

Note: Cont with A until it runs out, and then work part rounds with B and C to enhance random effect.

Round 1: ch2, 1sc into each hdc to end, ch2 (for corner), working evenly in sc (working approx 4sc to every 3 row ends) along side edge of rug, ch2, 1sc into each loop along other side of Foundation row, ch2, work evenly in sc along other side edge, join with a sl st into 2ch sp.

Rounds 2 and 3: Work (1sc, ch2, 1sc) into 2ch sp at each corner and 1sc into each sc of previous round, join with a sl st into first sc. Fasten off.

Matching hat and scarf

Beat the chill in this cozy combination of pull-on hat and short scarf.

This complementary set of hat and matching scarf is worked in a beautiful alpaca yarn. The plain, wide double crochet stitch pattern is offset by attractive details in a harmonizing color—a looped edging on the scarf and staggered stripes on the hat.

GETTING STARTED

★★ *Easy fabric for scarf and hat, but decorative touches require practice.*

Size:

Scarf: 7 x 40 inches wide (18 x 100cm) long (excluding edging)

Hat: 22 inches (56cm) circumference

How much yarn:

Scarf: 3 x 50g (1¾oz) balls of Artesano 100% Alpaca DK in color A—Bolivia (shade 0785)

1 ball in color B—Anemone (shade C986)

Hat: 2 x 50g (1¾oz) balls of Artesano 100% Alpaca DK in color A—Bolivia (shade 0785)

1 ball in color B—Anemone (shade C986)

Note: Set takes 4 balls A and 1 ball B

Hook:

4.00mm (G/6) crochet hook

Gauge:

16 sts and 10 rows measure 4 inches (10cm) square over wide dc patt on 4.00mm (G/6) hook

IT IS ESSENTIAL TO WORK TO THE STATED GAUGE TO ACHIEVE SUCCESS.

What you have to do:

Work scarf main section in wide double crochet pattern. Work pendant edging at ends in contrast color. Work crown of hat in wide double crochet pattern increasing as instructed. Work straight for sides, adding contrast-color stripes. Work surface crochet over final rounds.

The Yarn

Artesano Alpaca DK (approx. 100m/109 yards per 50g/1¾oz ball) contains pure superfine alpaca. It is a soft luxurious DK yarn. Handwash only, there are plenty of neutral and colorful shades.

Instructions

Abbreviations:

ch = chain
cm = centimeter(s)
cont = continue
dc = double crochet
dcb = inserting hook from back and from right to left, work 1dc around stem of next tr
foll = follows
hdc = half double crochet
mm = millimeter(s)
patt = pattern
rep = repeat
RS = right side
sc = single crochet
sl st = slip stitch
sp(s) = space(s)
st(s) = stitch(es)
WS = wrong side
yo = yarn over hook

SCARF:

With A, ch29 loosely.

Row 1: (WS) 1dc in 4th ch from hook, 1dc in each ch to end, turn. 27 sts.

Cont in wide tr patt working into sps between sts as foll:

Patt row: ch2, *1dc in sp before next tr, rep from * ending 1dc in sp before turning ch, turn.

Rep patt row until work measures 40 inches (100cm), ending with a WS row. Fasten off.

Pendant edging:

With RS facing, join B in sp between 1st and 2nd sts of last row, ch1, 1sc in same place, ch12, sl st in 3rd ch from sc to form a ring, (1sc, 1hdc, 12dc, 1hdc, 1sc) in ring, sl st in same ch as last sl st—pendant worked, ch3, skip 4 sps of last row, 1sc in next sp, *ch12, sl st in 3rd ch from sc to form a ring, (1sc, 1hdc and 1dc) in ring,

drop loop from hook, insert hook in 11th of 12dc of last pendant, replace loop on hook and pull through 11th of 12dc, now work (11dc, 1hdc and 1sc) in same ring, sl st in same ch as last sl st—pendant worked, ch3, skip 4 sps of last row, 1sc in next sp, rep from * 3 times.
Fasten off.

Work pendant edging along other end.

HAT:
Crown:

Round 1: With A, ch4, 9dc in 4th ch from hook, sl st in 3rd of 3ch. 10 sts.

Cont in wide dc patt working into sps between sts as foll:

Round 2: ch2, 1dc in first sp, (2dc in next sp) 9 times, sl st in 2nd of 2ch. 20 sts.

Round 3: ch2, 1dc in first sp, 1dc in next sp, (2dc in next sp, 1dc in next sp) 9 times, sl st in 2nd of 2ch. 30 sts.

Round 4: ch2, 1dc in first sp, 1dc in each of next 2 sps, (2dc in next sp, 1dc in each of next 2 sps) 9 times, sl st in 2nd of 2ch. 40 sts.

Round 5: ch2, 1dc in first sp, 1dc in each of next 3 sps, (2dc in next sp, 1dc in each of next 3 sps) 9 times, sl st in 2nd of 2ch. 50 sts.

Round 6: ch2, 1dc in first sp, 1dc in each of next 4 sps, (2dc in next sp, 1dc in each of next 4 sps) 9 times, sl st in 2nd of 2ch. 60 sts.

Round 7: ch2, 1dc in first sp, 1dc in each of next 5 sps, (2dc in next sp, 1dc in each of next 5 sps) 9 times, sl st in 2nd of 2ch. 70 sts.

Round 8: ch2, 1dcb around stem of each dc, sl st in 2nd of 2ch.

Sides:

Round 9: ch2, 1dc in first sp, 1dc in each of next 6 sps, (2dc in next sp, 1dc in each of next 6 sps) 9 times, sl st in 2nd of 2ch. 80 sts.

Round 10: ch2, 1dc in first sp, 1dc in each of next 7 sps, (2dc in next sp, 1dc in each of next 7 sps) 9 times, sl st in 2nd of 2ch. 90 sts.

Round 11: ch2, 1dc in first sp, 1dc in each sp to last sp, skip last sp, sl st in 2nd of 2ch.

Rounds 12–17: As Round 11. Do not fasten off, but carry yarn loosely up back of work. Join in B.

Round 18: With B, as Round 11.

Round 19: With A, as Round 11.

Round 20: With B, as Round 11.

Round 21–23: With A, as Round 11.

Surface crochet:

Take care to work surface crochet at same gauge as Hat. Turn Hat 90° so that rounds are vertical, not horizontal. Instead of working from right to left, work up last round as foll: hold A on WS, insert hook into first sp between sts, yo and draw loop through to RS, *insert hook through next sp between sts, yo and draw loop through to RS and through loop on hook, rep from * to end. Fasten off.

With A, work a row of surface crochet on next round of wide dc patt. Miss next round. With B, work a row of surface crochet on Rounds 18 and 20.

Fasten off.

Color-block throw

Bright bold colors are used to great effect in this simple yet dramatic throw.

These large square motifs, worked in Aran yarn and a fabulous array of contrasting colors, each bordered in cream, make a great visual impact when sewn together into a throw.

GETTING STARTED

Squares are easy to work, but care is needed with assembly and border for a professional finish.

Size:
Finished throw measures 60 x 41 inches
(154 x 104cm)

How much yarn:
Debbie Bliss Rialto Aran
5 x 50g (1¾oz) balls in each of colors A—Light Green (shade 10) and B—Light Blue (shade 23)
4 balls in each of colors C—Fuchsia (shade 27); D—Dark Blue (shade 11); E—Red (shade 18) and F—Cream (shade 16)
1 ball in color G—Dark Green (shade 09)

Hook:
5.00mm (H/8) crochet hook

Gauge:
First 4 rounds measure 4 inches (10cm) square and completed square measures 10 inches (25cm) square on 5.00mm (H/8) hook
IT IS ESSENTIAL TO WORK TO THE STATED GAUGE TO ACHIEVE SUCCESS.

What you have to do:
Make a square motif in main color and rounds of double crochet with chain spaces at corners. Work final round in contrast color and single crochet. Make 24 squares in total in six different colors. Sew squares together, then work border in contrast color.

The Yarn
Debbie Bliss Rialto Aran (approx. 80m/87 yards per 50g/1¾oz ball) contains 100% extra-fine merino wool. It produces a soft, luxurious fabric, yet is easy to look after. There is a fantastic range of shades suitable for color work.

Instructions

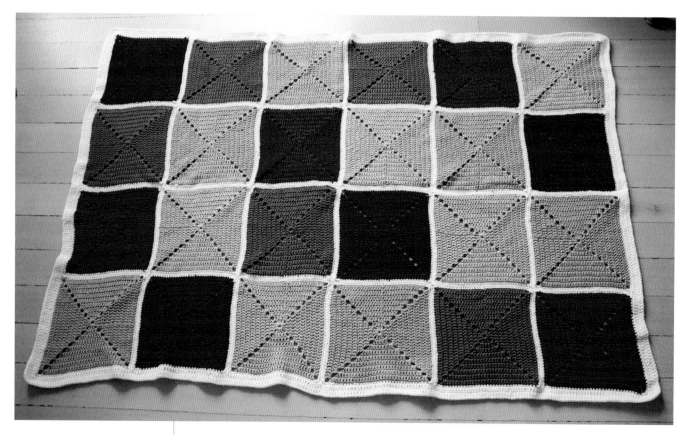

Abbreviations:

ch = chain
cm = centimeter(s)
dc = double crochet
rep = repeat
RS = right side
sc = single crochet
sl st = slip stitch
sp = space
st(s) = stitch(es)

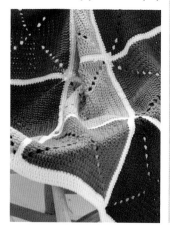

THROW:
Square:
With main color (A, B, C, D, E, or G), ch5, join with a sl st into first ch to form a ring.
Round 1: ch3 (counts as first dc), 2dc into ring, ch2, *3dc into ring, ch2, rep from * twice more, join with a sl st into 3rd of 3ch.
Round 2: ch3, skip st at base of ch, 1dc into each of next 2dc, *(1dc, ch3 and 1dc) into next 2ch sp, 1dc into each of next 3dc, rep from * twice more, (1dc, ch3 and 1dc) into next 2ch sp, join with a sl st into 3rd of 3ch.
Round 3: ch3, skip st at base of ch, 1dc into each of next 3dc, *(2dc, ch3 and 2dc) into next 3ch sp, 1dc into each of next 5dc, rep from * twice more, (2dc, ch3 and 2dc) into next 3ch sp, 1dc into next dc, join with a sl st into 3rd of 3ch.
Round 4: ch3, skip st at base of ch, 1dc into each of next 5dc, *(2dc, ch3 and 2dc)

into next 3ch sp, 1dc into each of next 9dc, rep from * twice more, (2dc, ch3 and 2dc) into next 3ch sp, 1dc into each of next 3dc, join with a sl st into 3rd of 3ch.
Round 5: ch3, skip st at base of ch, 1dc into each of next 7dc, *(2dc, ch3 and 2dc) into next 3ch sp, 1dc into each of next 13dc, rep from * twice more, (2dc, ch3 and 2dc) into next 3ch sp, 1dc into each of next 5dc, join with a sl st into 3rd of 3ch.
Round 6: ch3, skip st at base of ch, 1dc into each of next 9dc, *(2dc, ch3 and 2dc) into next 3ch sp, 1dc into each of next 17tr, rep from * twice more, (2dc, ch3 and 2dc) into next 3ch sp, 1dc into each of next 7dc, join with a sl st into 3rd of 3ch.
Round 7: ch3, skip st at base of ch, 1dc into each of next 11dc, *(2dc, ch3 and 2dc) into next 3ch sp, 1dc into each of next 21tr, rep from * twice more, (2dc, ch3 and 2dc) into next 3ch sp, 1dc into each of next 9dc, join with a sl st into 3rd of 3ch.

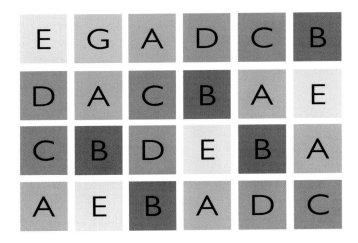

 Finishing

Lay the squares out, RS up, in 4 rows of 6 each, arranging colors as shown in diagram. Starting at top row, sew the first square to next along side edges, sliding needle under 2 loops at top of each sc on both squares. Add next 4 squares in the same way, then make up other 3 rows in same way. Finally, sew 4 rows together as before.

Border:

With RS facing, join F to first of 5sc at one corner, ch3, 1dc into next sc, *3dc into next sc (center of 5sc), 1dc into each sc to center of 5sc at next corner, rep from * twice more, 3dc into next sc, 1dc into each sc to end, join with a sl st into 3rd of 3ch.

Next round: ch3, skip st at base of ch, 1dc into each of next 2dc, *3dc into next dc (center of 3dc), 1dc into each dc to center of 3dc at next corner, rep from * twice more, 3dc into next dc, 1dc into each dc to end, join with a sl st into 3rd of 3ch. Fasten off.

Round 8: ch3, skip st at base of ch, 1dc into each of next 13dc, *(2dc, ch3 and 2dc) into next 3ch sp, 1dc into each of next 25tr, rep from * twice more, (2dc, ch3 and 2dc) into next 3ch sp, 1dc into each of next 11dc, join with a sl st into 3rd of 3ch.

Round 9: ch3, skip st at base of ch, 1dc into each of next 15dc, *(2dc, ch3 and 2dc) into next 3ch sp, 1dc into each of next 29tr, rep from * twice more, (2dc, ch3 and 2dc) into next 3ch sp, 1dc into each of next 13dc, join with a sl st into 3rd of 3ch. Fasten off.

Round 10: Join F to any ch3 sp, ch1 (does not count as a st), *5sc into 3ch sp, 1sc into each of next 33dc, rep from * 3 more times, join with a sl st into first sc. Fasten off, leaving a 20-inch (50-cm) length of yarn for sewing squares together.

Make 24 squares in total in the following colors, always using F for the last round:

6 in A, 5 in B, 4 in C, 4 in D, 4 in E, and 1 in G.

Two-color fingerless mitts

Team soft cream with brown yarn to make these cosy fingerless mitts.

These long mitts are worked mainly in single crochet in a soft, luxurious yarn and change color at the wrist with a decorative band of an openwork pattern.

The Yarn

Rowan Baby Alpaca DK (approx. 100m/109 yards per 50g/1¾oz ball) contains 100% baby alpaca. It produces a luxurious fabric that is handwash only. There is a good color palette including subtle natural shades and some deep colors.

GETTING STARTED

Simple project to practice working in rounds; thumb and finger shaping takes concentration.

Size:
To fit an average woman's hand; width around palm, 7 inches (18cm)

How much yarn:
2 x 50g (1¾oz) balls of Rowan Baby Alpaca DK in each of two colors: A—Cheviot (shade 207) and B—Jacob (shade 205)

Hook:
4.00mm (G/6) crochet hook

Gauge:
18 sts and 24 rows measure 4 inches (10cm) square over sc on 4.00mm (G/6) hook
IT IS ESSENTIAL TO WORK TO THE STATED GAUGE TO ACHIEVE SUCCESS.

What you have to do:
Work cuff section in first color and rounds of single crochet. Change to second color at wrist and work a decorative band of double crochet and chain spaces. Continue hand in rounds of single crochet, shaping for thumb and fingers as instructed. Work frill along foundation edge of cuffs.

Instructions

Abbreviations:

beg = beginning
ch = chain
cm = centimeter(s)
cont = continue
dc = double crochet
foll = follow(s)(ing)
inc = increase
patt = pattern
rep = repeat
RS = right side
sc = single crochet
sl st = slip stitch
sp = space
st(s) = stitch(es)
WS = wrong side

RIGHT MIT:

With A, ch35.

Foundation round: 1sc into 2nd ch from hook, 1sc into each ch to end, join with a sl st into first sc, turn. 34 sts.

Working in rounds but turning work at end of each round, cont as foll:

Patt round: 1sc into each st to end, join with a sl st into first sc, turn.

Rep last round until work measures 4¼ inches (11cm) from beg. Fasten off A and join in B to same place. Cont in B only, work wristband as foll:

Round 1: ch4 (counts as 1dc and 1ch), skip st at base of ch and foll st, 1dc into next st, *ch1, skip next st, 1dc into next st, rep from * to end, finishing ch1, skip next st, join with a sl st into 3rd of 4ch, turn.

Round 2: ch3 (counts as first dc), 1dc into first sp, *1dc into next dc, 1dc into next sp, rep from * to end, join with a sl st into 3rd of 3ch, turn.

Round 3: As Round 1.

Round 4: 1sc into first sp, 1sc into next tr, *1sc into next sp, 1sc into next tr, rep from * to end, join with a sl st into first sc, turn. 34 sts.

Cont in sc until work measures 4 inches (10cm) from beg of wristband.

Thumb round 1: (RS) 1sc into first sc, ch8, skip next 8 sts for thumb opening, patt to end, join with a sl st into first sc, turn.

2nd thumb round: 1sc into each of

next 25 sts, 1sc into each of next ch8, 1sc into last st, join with a sl st into first sc, turn. 34 sts.

Cont in patt until work measures 1½ inches (4cm) from beg of thumb opening, ending with a WS row.

First finger:

Next round: (RS) 1sc into each of first 4 sts, 2sc into next st, skip next 24 sts, 2sc into next st, 1sc into each of last 4 sts, join with a sl st into first sc, turn. 12 sts.

Patt 6 rounds on these 12 sts. Fasten off.

Second finger:

With RS facing, join B to same st as first inc on first finger, ch1 (counts as first sc), 1sc into each of next 4 sts, 2sc into next st, skip next 14 sts, 2sc into next st, 1sc into each of next 4 sts, 1sc into same sc as second inc on first finger, join with a sl st into first ch, turn. 14 sts.

Patt 8 rounds on these 14 sts. Fasten off.

Third finger:

With RS facing, join B to same st as first inc on second finger, ch1, 1sc into each of next 3 sts, 2sc into next st, skip next 6 sts, 2sc into next st, 1sc into each of next 3 sts, 1sc into same sc as second inc on second finger, join with a sl st into first ch, turn. 12 sts.

Patt 6 rounds on these 14 sts. Fasten off.

Fourth finger:

With RS facing, join B to same st as first inc on third

finger, ch1, 1sc into same st, 1sc into each of next 6 sts, 2sc into same st as second inc on third finger, join with a sl st into first ch, turn. 10 sts.

Patt 4 rounds on these 10 sts. Fasten off.

Thumb:

With RS facing, join B to first st at thumb opening and work ch1 (counts as first sc), 1sc into each st and 1sc into each ch around opening, join with a sl st into first ch. 16 sts.

Patt 6 rounds on these 16 sts. Fasten off.

Frill:

With RS of work facing, join A to first foundation ch and work ch3 (counts as first tr), 3dc into first ch, 4dc into each ch to end, join with a sl st into 3rd of 3ch. Fasten off.

LEFT MITT:

Work as given for Right Mitt but working 2 thumb rounds as foll:

Thumb round 1: (RS) 1sc into each of first 25 sts, ch8, skip next 8 sts for thumb opening, 1sc into last st, join with a sl st into first sc, turn.

Thumb round 2: 1sc into first st, 1sc into each of next ch8, 1sc into each st to end, join with a sl st into first sc, turn. 34 sts.

Cable hot-water bottle cover

The cable pattern on this cover gives it extra snuggle appeal.

Make sure your weekend guest stays warm even if your house is cold by providing her (or him) with a hot water bottle in this luxurious cover.

The Yarn

Debbie Bliss Andes (approx. 100m/109 yards per 50g/1¾oz ball) is a blend of 65% baby alpaca and 35% mulberry silk. It produces a luxurious soft, silky fabric. It is handwash only. There is a good range of colors.

GETTING STARTED

★ ★ *Not much shaping involved but working cable pattern requires concentration.*

Size:
To fit a hot-water bottle measuring 8 x 14 inches (20 x 35cm)

How much yarn:
4 x 50g (1¾oz) balls of Debbie Bliss Andes in Pale Blue (shade 11)

Hook:
4.00mm (G/6) crochet hook

Additional items:
3 buttons, ¾ inch (2cm) in diameter
Piece of cardboard or pom pom maker

Gauge:
19 sts and 13 rows measure 4 inches (10cm) square over patt on 4.00mm (G/6) hook
IT IS ESSENTIAL TO WORK TO THE STATED GAUGE TO ACHIEVE SUCCESS.

What you have to do:
Work in cable pattern with relief double crochet throughout, making buttonhole band in single crochet. Work mock ribbing with relief double crochet for top of cover. Make a twisted cord and trim with pom poms to tie around neck of cover.

Instructions

Abbreviations:

beg = beginning
ch = chain(s)
cm = centimeter(s)
cont = continue
cross 6 = skip next 3 sts, work 1rdcf around stem of each of next 3 sts, now working in front of last 3 sts work 1rdcf around stems of 3 skipped sts, beg at original first st
dc = double crochet
dc2tog = (yo, insert hook into next st and draw a loop through, yo and draw through first 2 loops on hook) twice, yo and draw through all 3 loops on hook
foll = follows
mm = millimeter(s)
patt = pattern
rep = repeat
rdcb = relief tr back as foll: yo, insert hook from back and from right to left around stem of next st, yo and draw a loop through, complete dc in usual way
rdcf = relief tr front as foll: yo, insert hook from front and from right to left around stem of next st, yo and draw a loop through, complete dc in usual way
sl st = slip stitch
sp = space
st(s) = stitch(es)
tr = triple
yo = yarn over hook

LOWER FRONT FLAP AND BACK: (Worked in one piece)
Ch39.

Buttonhole band:
Row 1: (RS) 1sc into 2nd ch from hook, 1sc in each ch to end, turn. 38 sts.
Row 2: ch1 (does not count as a st), 1sc in each of first 8 sts, (2ch, skip 2 sts, 1sc in each of next 8 sts) 3 times, turn.
Row 3: ch1, 1sc in each st and 2sc in each 2ch sp to end, turn.

Row 4: ch3 (counts as first tr), skip st at base of ch, 1dc in each st to end, turn. Cont in cable patt as foll:
Row 1: (RS) ch2 (counts as first tr), skip st at base of ch, 1dc in next st, 1rdcf around stem of next st, 1dc in each of next 2 sts, (1rdcf around stem of next 6 sts, 1dc in each of next 2 sts, 1rdcf around stem of next st, 1dc in each of next 2 sts) 3 times, working last tr in top of turning ch, turn.

Row 2: ch2, skip st at base of ch, 1dc in next st, 1rdcb around stem of next st, 1dc in each of next 2 sts, (1rdcb around stem of next 6 sts, 1dc in each of next 2 sts, 1rdcb around stem of next st, 1dc in each of next 2 sts) 3 times, working last tr in top of turning ch, turn.

Rows 3 and 4: As Rows 1 and 2.

Row 5: ch2, skip st at base of ch, 1dc in next st, 1rdcf around stem of next st, 1dc in each of next 2 sts, (cross 6, 1dc in each of next 2 sts, 1rdcf around stem of next st, 1dc in each of next 2 sts) 3 times, working last tr in top of turning ch, turn.

Row 6: As Row 2, taking care to work 6 crossed sts in their new order. Insert markers at each end of last row to denote lower back edge of cover. The last 6 rows form patt. Rep them 5 more times, then work Rows 1 and 2 again.

Shape top:

Next row: ch2, skip st at base of ch, dc2tog over next 2 sts, patt to last 3 sts, dc2tog over next 2 sts, 1dc in top of turning ch, turn.

Rep last row 3 more times. 30 sts. Fasten off.

FRONT:

With 4.00mm (G/6) hook make 39ch.

Row 1: (RS) 1sc in 2nd ch from hook, 1sc in each ch to end, turn. 38 sts.

Rows 2 and 3: ch1 (does not count as a st), 1sc in each st to end, turn.

Row 4: ch3 (counts as first tr), skip st at base of ch, 1dc in each st to end, turn. Cont in cable patt as given for Lower Front Flap and back until 32 rows have been worked.

Shape top:

Work as given for Lower Front Flap and back, but do not fasten off.

Next row: Sl st in each of next 6 sts, do not fasten off but leave on one side for working ribbing.

Finishing

Ribbing:

With RS facing, join shaped seams at top for both pieces and 6 sts at each side of top edge. With yarn left at end of Front, work in rib patt around top edge as foll:

Next round: ch2 (does not count as a st), (1rdcf around stem of next st, 1rdcb around stem of next st) 9 times across center front and 9 times across center back, join with a sl st in first rdcf. 36 sts. Rep last round until ribbing measures 2¾ inches (7cm) from beg. Fasten off. With RS of both pieces facing, join side seams, folding back along marked edge so that lower front flap is under main piece of front. Turn RS out and sew on buttons to match buttonholes.

Make a twisted cord approximately 35 inches (90cm) long and sew center of cord to center back of cover at base of ribbing. Make 2 pom poms (see Finishing instructions on page 63) and sew one to each end of cord. Tie cord in a neat bow around neck of cover.

Crochet hook roll

Have all sizes of crochet hook on hand with this
practical roll-up case.

Keep your crochet hooks handy in this easy-to-make crochet case worked in a variegated yarn with a fabric lining. Just roll the case up and secure with crochet ties decorated with flower motifs.

GETTING STARTED

★ ★ *Crocheted main piece is very easy, but a few simple sewing skills are necessary for lining the project.*

Size:
Case measures approximately 10 inches (25cm) wide x 8½ inches (22cm) high when unrolled

How much yarn:
1 x 100g (3½oz) ball of King Cole Mirage DK in color A—Nice (shade 873)
1 x 100g (3½oz) ball of King Cole Haze DK in color B—Damson (shade 456)

Hooks:
3.50mm (E/4) crochet hook
4.00mm (G/6) crochet hook

Additional items:
32 x 10 inches (80 x 25cm) piece of cotton lining fabric
Matching sewing thread

Gauge:
17 sts and 14 rows measure 4 inches (10cm) square over hdc on 4.00mm (G/6) hook
IT IS ESSENTIAL TO WORK TO THE STATED GAUGE TO ACHIEVE SUCCESS.

What you have to do:
Work main piece in half double crochet in variegated yarn. Work edging around main piece in single crochet and solid-colored yarn. Make chain and slip-stitch ties decorated with flower motifs. Sew separate fabric lining with pockets for hooks. Stitch lining on top of crochet main piece.

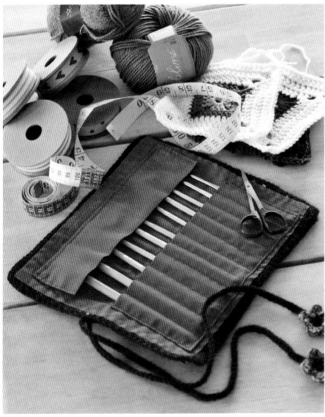

The Yarn
King Cole Mirage DK (approx. 312m/340 yards per 100g/3½oz ball) is 50% wool and 50% acrylic, and there's a good range of variegated colors. Use solid-colored King Cole Haze DK (approx. 488m/532 yards per 100g/ 3½oz ball)—a brushed 100% acrylic yarn—for edgings and ties.

Instructions

Abbreviations:

beg = beginning
ch = chain(s)
cm = centimeter(s)
dc = double crochet
hdc = half double crochet
mm = millimeters
patt = pattern
rep = repeat
sc = single crochet
RS = right side
sl st = slip stitch
st(s) = stitch(es)
WS = wrong side

MAIN PIECE:

With larger hook and A, ch40.

Foundation row: (RS) 1hdc into 3rd ch from hook, 1hdc into each ch to end, turn.

Patt row: ch2 (counts as first hdc), skip st at base of ch, 1hdc into each hdc to end, working last hdc into 2nd of 2ch, turn. 39 sts.

Rep last row to form patt until work measures 8 inches (20cm) from beg, ending with a WS row and changing to B on last part of last st in A.

Edging:

With B and RS facing, ch1 (counts as first st), skip st at base of ch, 1sc into each st across top edge, 3sc into corner st, 1sc into each row end down side, 3sc into corner st, 1sc into st along other side of foundation ch, 3sc into corner st, 1sc into each row end up other side, 3sc into corner st, join with a sl st into first ch. Work another round in sc, working 3sc into center of 3sc at each corner, join with a sl st into first ch. Fasten off.

TIES:

With larger hook and RS of work facing, join B halfway down one side edge of main piece and ch71.

*Next row: Sl st into 2nd ch from hook, sl st into each ch to end, then sl st into side edge of main piece *; ch71 and rep from * to *. Fasten off.

FLOWER MOTIFS: (make 2)

With smaller hook and B, make a magic circle (see Note on page 21), working ch1 and then working 5sc into the loop. Pull gently on the tail yarn to close the circle, change to A and join with a sl st into first ch.

Next round: *ch1, (1hdc, 1dc, 1hdc) into next sc, ch1, sl st into same sc, rep from *
4 more times. 5 petals made. Fasten off.

Sew a flower motif to end of each tie.

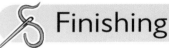 Finishing

Lining:

Cut a piece of fabric 10½ x 9 inches (27 x 23cm) for lining. Press under and machine-stitch ⅝ inches (1.5cm) on all edges, mitering the corners.

Cut a strip of lining fabric 9½ x 8¼ inches (24 x 21cm) for pocket. With RS facing, fold strip in half widthwise and stitch along one short end and long side, taking ⅝ inches (1.5cm) seam allowance. Trim seam, turn RS out, and press. Fold in seam allowances at other short edge, press and pin. With long seamed edge at bottom, pin this strip ¼ inch (5mm) from lower edge and centered between side edges of main lining piece and stitch along each side and across seamed edge to form a pocket. Then sew vertical lines, every ⅝ inches (1.5cm) apart for smaller hooks and ¾ inch (2cm) apart for larger hooks, through all thicknesses.

Cut another strip of lining fabric 10 x 5½ inches (25 x14cm) high for flap. With RS facing, fold strip in half widthwise and stitch along each short end, taking ⅝ inches (1.5cm) allowance and leaving long side open. Trim seams, turn RS out and press. Fold in seam allowances along long edge, press, and pin this edge in place ⅝ inches (1.5cm) from top edge of main lining piece. Stitch along pinned edge only to form a flap to protect hooks and stop them from slipping out of roll. With WS facing, pin lining, pocket, and flap piece to main crochet panel and slipstitch lining in place around all sides.

Zingy round pillow

Give your décor a color pop with this bright circular pillow.

This circular pillow with a shell edging has stitches with a pronounced spiral effect and funky shaded coloring created by working with two strands of yarn.

The Yarn

Patons Diploma Gold DK (approx. 131 yards/120m per 50g/1¾oz ball) is a blend of 55% wool, 25% acrylic, and 20% nylon. It combines wool's natural good looks with the easy-care properties of man-made fibers. It is machine washable, and there is a fantastic range of shades.

GETTING STARTED

 Working in a spiral with frequent color changes need constant attention.

Size:
16 inches (40cm) in diameter

How much yarn:
2 x 50g (1¾oz) balls of Patons Diploma Gold DK in each of four colors: A—Orange (shade 06304); B—Cherry (shade 06139); C—Cyclamen (shade 06123); D—Violet (shade 06242)

Hook:
7.00mm (K/10½) crochet hook

Additional items:
16 inches (40cm) round pillow with red slipcover
Small safety pins

Gauge:
First 3 rounds of front measure 4 inches (10cm) in diameter with two strands of yarn and 7.00mm (K/10½) hook (**Note:** subsequent rounds contract—every 4 rounds add 3½ inches (9cm) to diameter)
IT IS ESSENTIAL TO WORK TO THE STATED GAUGE TO ACHIEVE SUCCESS.

What you have to do:
Use 2 strands of yarn together throughout, changing colors at intervals to give a shaded effect. Work both sides of pillow in the round, starting at the center and working in a continuous spiral. After pillow has been inserted, work a shell edging around edge.

Instructions

Abbreviations:

ch = chain(s)
cm = centimeter(s)
dc = double crochet
hdc = half double crochet
mm = millimeter(s)
rep = repeat
sc = single crochet
sl st = slip stitch
st(s) = stitch(es)
yrh = yarn over hook

Notes:

Pillow is worked throughout using 2 strands of yarn together. Always join in new color on last part of last st worked in old color.

FRONT:

With 2 strands of A, ch6, join with a sl st in first ch to form a ring.
Round 1: ch2, 13dc in ring.
Note: In next and subsequent rounds, each st is worked around stem of dc rather than through 2 loops at top—work yo, insert hook from back and from right to left around stem of dc and draw loop through, complete dc in usual way.
Round 2: 2dc in 2nd of 2ch, (2dc in next dc) 13 times, insert a small safety pin in last st to mark end of round and move up on every round. 28tr.
Round 3: *2dc in next dc, 1dc in next dc *, rep from * to * twice more, cut off 1 strand of A and join in 1 strand of B, then rep from * to * to end. 42tr.
Round 4: *2dc in next dc, 1dc in each of next 2dc, rep from * to end. 56tr.
Round 5: *2dc in next dc, 1dc in each of next 3dc *, cut off strand of A and join in another strand of B, then rep from * to * to end. 70tr.
Round 6: *2dc in next dc, 1dc in each of

next 4dc, rep from * to end. 84tr.

Round 7: 1dc in each of next 35tr, cut off 1 strand of B and join in 1 strand of C, 1dc in each dc to end.

Round 8: *2dc in next dc, 1dc in each of next 5dc, rep from * to end. 98tr.

Round 9: 1dc in each of next 40tr, cut off strand of B and join in another strand of C, 1dc in each dc to end.

Round 10: *2dc in next dc, 1dc in each of next 6dc, rep from * to end. 112tr.

Round 11: 1dc in each of next 65tr, cut off 1 strand of C and join in 1 strand of D, 1dc in each dc to end.

Round 12: 1dc in each dc to end.

Round 13: *2dc in next dc, 1dc in each of next 7dc *, rep from * to * 4 more times, cut off strand of C and join in second strand of D, then rep from * to * to end. 126tr.

Round 14: 1dc in each of next 2dc, cut off 1 strand of D and join in 1 strand of A, 1dc in each dc to end.

Round 15: 1dc in each dc to end.

Round 16: *2dc in next dc, 1dc in each of next 8dc *, rep from * to * 5 more times, cut off strand of D and join in second strand of A, then rep from * to * to end. 140tr.

Round 17: 1dc in each of next 70tr, cut off 1 strand of A and join in 1 strand of B, 1dc in each dc to end.

Round 18: 1dc in each dc to end.

Round 19: 1dc in each of next 10dc, cut off strand of A and join in second strand of B, 1dc in each dc to end (to marker pin), 1hdc in next dc, 1sc in next dc. Fasten off.

BACK:

Wrap two strands of D 10 times round forefinger of left hand. Keeping hold of strands, remove "ring" from finger, insert 7.00mm (K/10½) hook into ring, yo and draw a loop through, ch2, work 14dc into ring, pull gently on end of yarn to close up ring.

Round 1: 2dc in 2nd of 2ch, (2dc in next dc) 14 times, insert a small safety pin in last st to mark end of round and move up on every round. 30tr.

Round 2: *2dc in next dc, 1dc in next dc *, rep from * to * 3 more times, cut off 1 strand of D and join in 1 strand of C, then rep from * to * to end. 45tr.

Round 3: *2dc in next dc, 1dc in each of next 2dc *, rep from * to * 4 more times, cut off strand of D and join in another strand of C, rep from * to * to end. 60tr.

Round 4: *2dc in next dc, 1dc in each of next 3dc *, rep from * to * 3 more times, cut off 1 strand of C and join in 1 strand of B, rep from * to * 3 times, cut off strand of C and join in 1 strand of A, rep from * to * to end. 75tr.

Round 5: 1dc in each of next 40tr, cut off strand of B, join in another strand of A, 1dc in each dc to end.

Round 6: *2dc in next dc, 1dc in each of next 4dc rep from * to end. 90tr.

Round 7: 1dc in each of next 12dc, cut off strand of A and join in 1 strand of D, 1dc in each dc to end.

Round 8: *2dc in next dc, 1dc in each of next 5dc *, rep from * to * 5 more times, cut off strand of A and join in another strand of D, rep from * to * to end (105tr), 1hdc in next tr, 1sc in next tr. Fasten off.

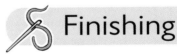 Finishing

Pin front panel to one side of pillow and back panel to the other side. Holding edges with small safety pins, slipstitch closed using 1 strand of yarn.

Edging:

With front of pillow facing, join 2 strands of C to any tr, sl st in same place as join, (skip next dc, 5dc in next dc, skip next 2dc, sl st in next tr) to end. Fasten off.

Book cover with handles

Keep your diary, sketchbook, or notebook inside this distinctive cover.

Give your notebook or diary an individual look with this cover in a textured woven stitch and stripes. It has a fabric lining and can be carried around with handles that are made separately and sewn on.

The Yarn
Debbie Bliss Cashmerino DK (approx. 110m/120 yards per 50g/1¾oz ball) contains 55% merino wool, 33% microfiber and 12% cashmere. It is a soft, luxurious yarn that is machine washable at a low temperature. The palette contains a lot of appealing shades.

GETTING STARTED

★★ *Attention needed, as fabric is constructed in a slightly unusual way.*

Size:
To fit an up to 8¼ x 6 inches (21 x 15cm) hardback notebook

How much yarn:
1 x 50g (1¾oz) ball of Debbie Bliss Cashmerino DK in each of 3 colors: A—Aqua (shade 28); B—Pink (shade 27); and C—Pistachio (shade 29)

Hook:
3.50mm (E/4) crochet hook

Additional items:
Two 10 x 5½ inches (25 x 14cm) pieces of medium-weight cotton fabric
Sewing needle and thread to match yarn A

Gauge:
15 sts and 19 rows measure 4 inches (10cm) square over pattern on 3.50mm (E/4) hook
IT IS ESSENTIAL TO WORK TO THE STATED GAUGE TO ACHIEVE SUCCESS.

What you have to do:
Work cover in textured woven pattern with stripes as instructed. Work handle in 2 colors in the same pattern. Sew fabric lining into cover.

 Instructions

BOOK COVER:

With A, 49ch very loosely.

Foundation row: (RS) Insert hook in 2nd ch from hook, yo and draw a loop through, insert hook in next ch, yo and draw a loop through, yo and draw through all 3 loops on hook, *insert hook in same ch as 2nd loop of previous st, yo and draw a loop through, insert hook in next ch, yo and draw a loop through, yo and draw through all 3 loops on hook, rep from * to end, 1sc in same ch as 2nd loop of previous st, turn. 48 sts.

Row 1: ch1 (does not count as a st), insert hook in first st, yo and draw through a loop, insert hook in next st, yo and draw through a loop, yo and draw through all 3 loops on hook, *insert hook in same st as 2nd loop

Abbreviations:
beg = beginning
ch = chain(s)
cm = centimeter(s)
dc = double crochet
mm = millimeter(s)
rep = repeat
RS = right side
sl st = slip stitch
st(s) = stitch(es)
yo = yarn over hook

of previous st, yo and draw through a loop, insert hook in next st, yo and draw through a loop, yo and draw through all 3 loops on hook, rep from * to end, 1sc in last st, remove hook from work, leaving loop on a safety pin, do not turn.

Row 2: Starting at beg of row just worked, join in B and work ch1, 1sc in first st, 1sc in each st to end, then remove safety pin and pull loop of A through loop on hook, turn but do not cut off B.

Row 3: ch1, insert hook in first st, yo and draw through a loop, insert hook in next st, yo and draw through a loop, yo, draw through all 3 loops on hook, *insert hook in same st as 2nd loop of previous st, yo and draw through a loop, insert hook in next st, yo and draw through a loop, yo and draw through all 3 loops on hook, rep from * to end, 1sc in last st, turn.

Row 4: As Row 3, changing to B on last st (do not cut A).

Row 5: With B, as Row 3.

Row 6: As Row 3, changing to A on last st; cut off B.

Row 7: With A, as Row 3.

Row 8: As Row 3.

Rows 9–13: ch1, 1sc in first st, 1sc in each st to end, turn.

Row 14: ch1, insert hook in first st, yo and draw through a loop, insert hook in next st, yo and draw through a loop, yo and draw through all 3 loops on hook, *insert hook in same st as 2nd loop of previous st, yo and draw through a loop, insert hook in next st, yo and draw through a loop, yo and draw through all 3 loops on hook, rep from * to end, 1sc in last st, remove hook from work, leaving loop on a safety pin, do not turn.

Row 15: Using C instead of B, as Row 2.

Row 16: As Row 3.

Row 17: As Row 3, changing to C on last st (do not cut off A).

Row 18: With C, as Row 3.

Row 19: As Row 3, changing to A on last st; cut off C.

Row 20: With A, as Row 3.

Rows 21–26: As 14th–19th rows.

Rows 27–31: ch1, 1sc in first st, 1sc in each st to end, turn.

Row 32: As Row 3.

Rows 33–39: As Rows 2–8.

Row 40: ch1, 1sc in first st, 1sc in each st to end. Fasten off.

HANDLES:

With B, ch160 very loosely, join with a sl st in first ch to form a ring.

Foundation round: ch1 (does not count as a st), insert hook in first ch, yo and draw through a loop, insert hook in next ch, yo and draw through a loop, yo and draw through all 3 loops on hook, * insert hook in same ch as 2nd loop of previous st, yo and draw through a loop, insert hook in next ch, yo and draw through a loop, yo and draw through all 3 loops on hook, rep from * to end, join with a sl st in first st.

Round 1: ch1 (does not count as st), insert hook in first st, yo and draw through a loop, insert hook in next st, yo and draw through a loop, yo and draw through all 3 loops on hook, * insert hook in same st as 2nd loop of previous st, yo and draw through a loop, insert hook in next st, yo and draw through a loop, yo and draw through all 3 loops on hook, rep from * to end, join with a sl st in first st, joining in C (do not cut off B).

Round 2: With C, as Round 1. Fasten off C.

3rd and 4th rounds: With B, as Round 1.

Round 5: Sl st in each st.

Round 6: Carrying yarn loosely across back of work, sl st in first ch of foundation ch and work 1ss in each st, join with a sl st in first st. Fasten off.

Finishing

Weave in all loose ends. Finish one long edge of each lining piece with a narrow double hem, then turn in ⅝ inches (1.5cm) on each of the remaining edges. Place each fabric lining piece RS up on inside of book cover and pin in place. Using matching sewing thread, overcast edge of book cover and folded edges of lining together to form pockets for hard covers of book.

Slip cover onto book. Press handle and pin, then stitch it in place as shown in photographs.

Gift charms

Take your wrapping to another level with these distinctive crochet charms.

Whatever the occasion, you can give a gift package a personal touch with these cute decorative charms, worked in single crochet.

GETTING STARTED

⭐ *Easy to make, but these tiny items require a lot of attention to detail.*

Size:
Each charm measures approximately 2¾–3½ inches (7–9cm) tall; test guage with the Heart and adjust hook size if necessary.

How much yarn:
1 x 25g (1oz) ball of Patons FaB DK in each of six colors: A—White (shade 02306); B—Green (shade 02329); C—Brown (shade 02309); D—Turquoise (shade 02315); E—Peach (shade 02303) and F—Red (shade 02323)

Hook:
4.00mm (G/6) crochet hook

Additional items:
Christmas tree: Polyester fiberfill; 8 inches (20cm) of ⅛ inch- (3mm-) wide green ribbon; star bead
Horseshoe: White pipe cleaner, 10 inches (25cm) long; 8 inches (20cm) of ⅛ in- (3mm-) wide white ribbon; 8 x ⅛ inches (11 x 6mm) pearl beads
Gift box: Polyester fiberfill; 8 inches (20cm) of ⅛ inch- (3mm-) wide white ribbon; 1 yard (90cm) of coordinating sheer blue ribbon
Starfish: Polyester fiberfill; 8 inches (20cm) of ⅛ inch- (3mm-) wide peach ribbon; 15 x ¼in (6mm) pearl beads
Heart: polyester fiberfill; 8 inches (20cm) of ⅛ inch- (3mm-) wide red ribbon

What you have to do:
Work each charm in single crochet. Shape and add stuffing as directed. Add decorative touches and a ribbon hanging loop to each charm as instructed.

The Yarn
Patons Fab DK (approx. 68m per 25g/1oz ball) is 100% acrylic. Good for toys, it is available in small balls and many colors.

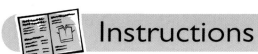 Instructions

CHRISTMAS TREE CHARM:
Tree body:
With B, make a magic circle as foll: Wind B several times around tip of left forefinger. Carefully slip ring off finger, insert hook into ring, pull yarn through and make ch1, then work 4sc in ring, join with a sl st in first sc. Pull end of yarn gently to close ring. 4 sts.
Marking beg of each round, work in continuous rounds with WS facing as foll: *
Round 1: 1sc in each st to end.
Round 2: 2sc in each st to end. 8 sts.
Round 3: (2sc in next st, 1sc in next st) to end. 12 sts.
Round 4: As Round 1.
Round 5: (2sc in next st, 1sc in each of next 2 sts) to end. 16 sts.
Round 6: As Round 1.
Round 7: (2sc in next st, 1sc in each of next 3 sts) to end. 20 sts.
Round 8: As Round 1.
Round 9: (Working in front loops only, sc2tog over next 2 sts) to end. 10 sts.
Rounds 10 and 11: As Rounds 1 and 2. 20 sts.
Round 12: (2sc in next st, 1sc in each of next 4 sts) to end. 24 sts.
Round 13: As Round 1.
Round 14: (2sc in next st, 1sc in each of next 5 sts) to end. 28 sts.
Round 15: As Round 1.

Abbreviations:

beg = beginning
ch = chain(s)
cm = centimeter(s)
cont = continue
dec = decreased
foll = follows
mm = millimeter(s)
rem = remains
rep = repeat
RS = right side
sc = single crochet
sc2tog = (insert hook in next st, yo and draw a loop through) twice, yo and draw through all 3 loops
sl st = slip stitch
st(s) = stitch(es)
WS = wrong side
yo = yarn over hook

Round 16: (2sc in next st, 1sc in each of next 6 sts) to end. 32 sts.
Round 17: As Round 9. 16 sts.
Round 18: As Round 9, but working in both loops. 8 sts. Stuff shape firmly, then work (dc2tog over next 2 sts) until gap is closed. Fasten off.

Tree trunk:

With C, make a magic circle (see page 97) and make ch1, then work 6sc in ring, join with a sl st in first sc. 6 sts.
Rounds 1–3: 1sc in each st to end. Fasten off, leaving a 12 inch (30cm) tail for sewing trunk to tree body.

Garlands:

With A, ch25. Fasten off, leaving a 12 inch (30cm) tail for sewing to upper tree tier. Make another 40ch garland for sewing to lower tree tier.

HORSESHOE CHARM:

With A, work as Christmas tree charm to *.
Rounds 1 and 2: 1sc in each st to end. 4 sts.
Round 3: 2sc in first st, 1sc in each of next 3 sts. 5 sts.
Round 4: 1sc in each st to end.
Round 5: 2sc in first st, 1sc in each of next 4 sts. 6 sts.

Rounds 6–37: 1sc in each st to end.
Round 38: Sc2tog over first 2 sts, 1sc in each of next 4 sts. 5 sts.
Round 39: 1sc in each st to end.
Round 40: Sc2tog over first 2 sts, 1sc in each of next 3 sts. 4 sts. Carefully insert pipe cleaner into center of tube and work rest of sts around end of pipe cleaner.
Rounds 41 and 42: 1sc in each st to end. Trim off excess pipe cleaner.
Round 43: (Sc2tog) twice. Fasten off.

GIFT BOX CHARM:

Top and base: (make 2)
With D, make ch8.
Foundation row: (RS) 1sc in 2nd ch from hook, 1sc in each ch to end, turn. 7 sts.
Rows 1–6: ch1 (counts as first sc), skip st at base of ch, 1sc in each st to end, turn. Fasten off.

Side panel:
With D, make ch14. Work Foundation row as top and base. 13 sts. Cont in rows of sc, working in stripes of 2 rows each D and A (always changing to new color on last part of last st in old color), until 28 rows in all have been completed.
Last row: Fold work in half with RS facing so foundation edge lines up with row just worked; now work to end in sc through adjacent pairs of sts to form an open tube. Fasten off. Turn tube RS out.

STARFISH CHARM: (Make 2

but do not fasten off at end of second piece.)
Worked with RS facing.
With E, work as Christmas Tree Charm to *, working 5sc instead of 4sc in circle. 5 sts.
Round 1: 2sc in each st to end. 10 sts.
Round 2: (2sc in next st, 1sc in next st) to end. 15 sts.
Round 3: (2sc in next st, 1sc in each of next 2 sts) to end. 20 sts.
Round 4: (1sc in next st, ch6, skip ch1, 1sc in each of next ch5, sl st in each of

next 3 sts) 5 times.
Round 5: 1sc in each st all around. Fasten off.

HEART CHARM: (Make 2 hearts in same way.)
First heart top curve:
With F, make a magic circle as for Christmas Tree Charm.
4 sts. Turn.
Row 1: ch1 (does not count as a st), (1sc in next st, 2sc
in next st) twice, turn. 6 sts.
Row 2: ch1, (1sc in each of next 2 sts, 2sc in next st)
twice. 8 sts. Fasten off.
Second heart top curve:
Make a second heart top curve in same way but do not
fasten off at end.
Join curves:
Next row: ch1, work 5sc along straight edge of heart
curve, then 5sc along straight edge of other heart curve,
turn. 10 sts.
Next row: ch1, 1sc in each st, turn.
Next row: ch1, 1sc in each st to last st, turn. 1 st dec.
Rep last row until 1 st rem. Fasten off.

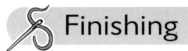 Finishing

CHRISTMAS TREE CHARM:
Stuff trunk and sew to middle of tree body base. Sew
garlands in place in loops of 5ch to each tree tier. Sew
star bead to top of tree. Thread ribbon through top of
tree, below star, and tie in a knot to make a hanging loop.

HORSESHOE CHARM:
Bend horseshoe into a U-shape. Spacing evenly, sew
beads onto one side of horseshoe. Thread ribbon
through center of top of horseshoe and tie in a knot to
make a hanging loop.

GIFT BOX CHARM:
Slipstitch base to one end of tube. Stuff well with fiberfill,
then slipstitch top in position. Tie coordinating ribbon
around gift box and tie in a bow on top of box. Thread
white ribbon through center of top of charm and tie in a
knot to make a hanging loop.

STARFISH CHARM:
With WS facing, place one starfish on top of the other,
now work in sc through adjacent pairs of sts around
edges to join, leaving a gap at end to insert filling. Stuff

firmly through gap and then cont in sc to close gap.
Fasten off. Sew one pearl bead to tip of each "arm" and
another 2 beads along arm. Thread ribbon through top of
one arm and tie in a knot to make a hanging loop.

HEART CHARM:
With WS facing, slipstitch hearts together around edges,
leaving a small gap for stuffing. Insert stuffing and then
close gap. Thread ribbon through center of curves at top
of heart and tie in a knot to make a hanging loop.

Laptop case

Protect your computer with this bright, funky cover.

Worked in easy single crochet and a bright, multicolored yarn, this zipped computer case has protective padding within its sewn lining.

The Yarn

King Cole Wicked DK (approx. 290m/316 yards per 100g/3½oz ball) contains 100% premium acrylic. This easy-care yarn has multicolored threads bound onto its solid background color; great for interesting patterns.

GETTING STARTED

 Easy fabric with no shaping, but a good result requires neat sewing and finishing.

Size:

Finished case measures approximately 15½ inches (39cm) wide x 10½ inches (27cm) high

How much yarn:

2 x 100g (3½oz) balls of King Cole Wicked DK in Black (shade 720)

Hook:

4.00mm (G/6) crochet hook

Additional items:

Pink zipper, 22 inches (56cm) long;
2 pieces of felt, each 14½ x 10 inches (37 x 25cm)
⅝ yard (60cm) of pink lining fabric 36 yard- (90cm-) wide

Matching sewing thread and needle

Gauge:

16.5 sts and 22 rows measure 4 inches (10cm) square over sc on 4.00mm (G/6) hook
IT IS ESSENTIAL TO WORK TO THE STATED GAUGE TO ACHIEVE SUCCESS.

What you have to do:

Work each side of case in single crochet, adding a single crochet edging all around. Add a single crochet zipper edging across top and partway down sides. Crochet back and front of case together on right side of work. Sew in zipper.
Add padding and sewn fabric lining.

Instructions

Abbreviations:

beg = beginning
ch = chain(s)
cm = centimeter(s)
mm = millimeter(s)
rep = repeat
RS = right side
sc = single crochet
sl st = slip stitch
st(s) = stitch(es)
tog = together
WS = wrong side

FRONT:

Ch62.

Foundation row: (RS) 1sc into 2nd ch from hook, 1sc into each ch to end, turn. 61sc.

Row 1: ch1 (does not count as a st), 1sc into each sc to end, turn. Rep last row until work measures 10 inches (25cm) from beg, ending with a WS row. Turn at end of final row but do not fasten off.

Edging:

With RS of Front facing, ch1 (does not count as a st), 1sc into each sc across top edge, 2sc into corner st, 1sc into each row end down side, 2sc into corner st, 1sc into each ch of other side of foundation ch, 2sc into corner st and 1sc into each row end up other side, 1sc into same place as first sc, join with a sl st into first sc.

Fasten off.

Zipper edging:

With RS of Front facing, join yarn to right-hand side 3 inches (8cm) down from top corner, ch1 (does not count as a st), 1sc into each sc up side, 2sc into corner st, 1sc into each sc across top edge, 2sc into corner st, 1sc into each sc down left side for 3 inches (8cm). Fasten off.

BACK:

Work as given for Front, but do not fasten off at end of zipper edging.

Joining Back and Front:

Place Back and Front with WS tog and zipper edging across top. With RS facing and using yarn attached, crochet pieces tog down first side, across lower edge and up second side to zipper edging by working 1sc through sc on both edges simultaneously and 2sc into each corner sc. Fasten off.

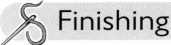

Finishing

Use finished case as a template to cut out 2 rectangles of pink lining fabric to same size as case. Sew in zipper down sides and across top of case between zipper edgings.

Lining:

Center 1 piece of felt on WS of each side of case and lightly slipstitch edges in place so that sts do not show through on RS. Turn under and press a ⅜-inch (1cm) hem along one long edge of each piece of lining fabric for top. With RS facing, beg and ending at point 3 inches (8cm) below fold, pin, then baste, side and lower edges. Slip lining inside crochet case to check size and adjust if necessary. Sew seam. Clip into corners. With WS facing, sew neatly to zipper tape.

Pastel patchwork bag

A really pretty variegated yarn is used for the patchwork squares in this lovely bag.

This practical square bag with a base and gussets is constructed from pretty patchwork motifs—all with the same variegated pastel shades in the center surrounded by a harmonizing solid color.

GETTING STARTED

★ ★ *Motifs are simple to make, but neat sewing is required to ensure a good finished result.*

Size:
Bag is 13 inches (33cm) wide x 13½ inches (34cm) high x 4¼ inches (11cm) deep, excluding handles

How much yarn:
2 x 100g (3½oz) skeins of Manos del Uruguay Fair Trade Wool Clasica in each of color A—Athena (shade 8931) and color B—Mississippi (shade 2370)

Hook:
5.00mm (H/8) crochet hook

Additional items:
1¾ yards (60cm) of 36-inch (90-cm) wide quilted fabric (see Note on page 106)
Sewing needle and matching thread

Gauge:
Each finished square measures 4¼ inches (11cm) on 5.00mm (H/8) hook
IT IS ESSENTIAL TO WORK TO THE STATED GAUGE TO ACHIEVE SUCCESS.

What you have to do:
Make square motifs in 2 colors—one variegated and one solid. Sew squares together to form bag. Make handles in rows of single crochet. Sew quilted lining for bag.

The Yarn
Manos del Uruguay Fair Trade Wool Clasica (approx. 126m/137 yards per 100g/3½oz ball) is a blend of Corriedale and Merino wool. It is handwash only.

Instructions

Abbreviations:

ch = chain
cm = centimeter(s)
cont = continue
dc = double crochet
foll = follows
mm = millimeter(s)
RS = right side
sc = single crochet
sl st = slip stitch
sp = space
WS = wrong side

Note: If you can buy ready-quilted fabric, with a layer of batting between two outer layers of fabric, choose one that is not too bulky. To make your own, sandwich layers of fabric and batting and machine-stitch diagonal lines through all layers to form a diamond-patterned grid of quilting stitches.

SQUARE MOTIF: (make 27)
With A, ch5, join with a sl st into first ch to form a ring.

Round 1: ch5, (3dc into ring, ch2) 3 times, 2dc into ring, join with a sl st into 3rd of 5ch.

Round 2: Sl st into next ch sp, ch7, (2dc into sp, 1dc into each of next 3dc, 2dc into next sp, ch4) 3 times, 2dc into sp, 1dc into each of next 3dc, 1dc into next sp, join with a sl st into 3rd of 7ch, changing to B.

Round 3: With B, sl st into next ch sp, (5sc into ch sp, 1sc into each of next 7dc) 4 times, join with a sl st into first sc.

Round 4: 1sc into each of first 2sc, (3sc into next sc, 1sc into each of next 11sc) 3

times, 3sc into next sc, 1sc into each of last 9sc, join with a sl st into first sc. Fasten off.

BAG:

Darn in ends, then press squares under a slightly damp cloth with a warm iron. Sew squares together to make 9 rows with 3 squares in each, then join 7 rows together to form bag front, base and back. Sew in 2 remaining rows to form side gussets.

Border:

With RS facing, join B to one side seam at top edge and cont as foll:

Round 1: ch1 (does not count as a st), 1sc into each sc along squares and 1sc in each seam end between squares, join with a sl st in first sc. 128sc.

Round 2: ch1, working into back loop only of each st, work 1sc into each sc to end, join with a sl st into first sc.

Rounds 3 and 4: Work in sc, inserting hook into both loops of each st as usual. Fasten off.

HANDLE: (make 2)

With B, leave a tail of at least 8 inches (20cm), then make ch59.

Foundation row: 1sc into 2nd ch from hook, 1sc into each ch to end, turn. 58 sts.

Rows 1–3: ch1 (does not count as a st), 1sc into each sc to end, turn.

Row 4: ch1, working into back loop only of each st, 1sc

into each sc to end, turn.

Rows 5–7: As Rows 1–3. Fold handle in half, along top of Row 3 and join each st of Row 7 to corresponding ch at opposite edge with a row of ss. Fasten off, leaving a long tail.

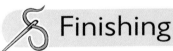 Finishing

Fold top border to inside and pin in place. Flatten bag and cut a rectangle of lining fabric to fit all around bag, allowing ⅝ inches (1.5cm) extra all around. With WS of fabric together, sew side seams ¼ inch (6mm) in from edges, then turn so that RS are together and stitch side seams again, ⅜ inch (9mm) from folded edges and trapping raw edges inside. Flatten corners and fold upward against side seam, then stitch across corners to form gusset. Trim off excess fabric at corners. Place lining inside bag, matching side seams and tucking raw edge under fold of bag border. Pin in place, then slipstitch edge of bag border to lining. Using picture as a guide to positioning, sew on handles to inside of border, stitching neatly through inner border, lining, and outer border.

Long gloves with a bow

Wear these long gloves pulled up or ruched down to suit your outfit. Either way they'll keep your fingers warm.

Worked in rounds of simple stitches with a rib effect at the cuff, these gloves feature a decorative band of surface crochet with ties at the wrist.

GETTING STARTED

★★★ *These gloves use simple stitches, but you will need to be accurate on the stitch count when working fingers and thumb.*

Size:
Around palm: 8 inches (20cm)
Length: 16 inches (40cm)
How much yarn:
3 x 50g (1¾oz) balls of King Cole Merino Blend 4-Ply in color A—Gray (shade 36)
1 ball in color B—Pink (shade 787)
Hooks:
3.00mm (C/2) crochet hook
2.00mm (3 steel) crochet hook
Gauge:
25 sts and 18 rows measure 4 inches (10cm) over patt on 3.00mm (C/2) hook
IT IS ESSENTIAL TO WORK TO THE STATED GAUGE TO ACHIEVE SUCCESS.
What you have to do:
Work in alternate rounds of single and double crochet. Add contrasting bands of surface crochet at wrist, finished with short single crochet ties. Shape for thumb and fingers as directed. Work a single row of crochet rib at top edge.

The Yarn
King Cole Merino Blend 4-Ply (approx. 180m/ 196 yards per 50g/1¾oz ball) contains 100% pure new wool in a machine-washable form. It is available in a wide range of colors and produces a soft, yet practical, fabric.

 Instructions

RIGHT GLOVE:
With larger hook and A, ch58, join with a sl st in first ch to form a ring taking care not to twist ch.
Foundation round: ch1 (does not count as a st), 1sc in same ch as sl st, 1sc in each ch to end, join with a sl st in first sc, turn. 58 sts.
Patt round 1: (RS) ch3 (counts as first dc), skip st at base of ch, 1dc in each st to end, join with a sl st in 3rd of 3ch, turn. Always work with RS outside—sc rounds are worked around inside (WS) of glove.

Patt round 2: ch1, 1sc in same place as sl st, 1sc in each st to end, join with a sl st in first sc, turn.
These 2 rounds form patt. Patt 6 more rounds.
Dec round 1: ch3, skip st at base of ch, 1dc in each of next 4 sts, dc2tog, 1dc in each of next 15 sts, dc2tog, 1dc in each of next 10 sts, dc2tog, 1dc in each of next 15 sts, dc2tog, 1dc in each of last 5 sts, join with a sl st in top of 3ch, turn. 54 sts.
Patt 9 rounds.
Dec round 2: ch3, skip st at base of ch, 1dc in each of

Abbreviations:
beg = beginning
ch = chain
cm = centimeter(s)
cont = continue
dc = double crochet
dc2tog = (insert hook in next st, yo and draw loop through) twice, yo and draw through all 3 loops
dec = decrease
foll = following
inc = increase(d)(s)
mm = millimeter(s)
patt = pattern
rem = remaining
rep = repeat
RS = right side
sp = space
sl st = slip stitch
st(s) = stitch(es)
tr = treble
tr2(3)tog = (yo, insert hook in next st, yo and draw loop through, yo and draw through first 2 loops) 2(3) times, yo and draw through all 3(4) loops
WS = wrong side
yo = yarn over hook

next 3 sts, dc2tog, 1dc in each of next 15 sts, dc2tog, 1dc in each of next 8 sts, dc2tog, 1dc in each of next 15 sts, dc2tog, 1dc in each of last 4 sts, join with a sl st in top of 3ch, turn. 50 sts.
Patt 13 rounds, ending with a Patt round 2.

Wristband:
Wrist round 1: As Patt round 1.
Wrist round 2: As Patt round 1 but work around inside (WS) of glove.
Wrist round 3: As Patt round 1.
Wrist round 4: As Patt round 2.
Slip working loop on a safety pin to prevent it from unraveling. Do not fasten off A.
Surface crochet: Holding yarn on WS (inside of work), attach B to ch3 at beg of Wrist round 1, insert hook in sp between last dc of round and 3ch at beg, yo and draw loop through, *insert hook in sp between 3ch and next dc, yo and pull loop through and through loop on hook, rep from * into each sp between sts to end, then work another round into

the same round of the wristband at the left of the first. At the end of the second round, insert hook, yo and pull loop through. Cut yarn leaving 40 inches (100cm) end for tie.
Ties: Insert hook through join of surface crochet, yo and draw loop through, (ch10, 1sc in 2nd ch from hook, 1sc in each ch, 1sl st in join of surface crochet) twice. Fasten off. Work 2 rounds of surface crochet around 2nd wrist round but do not work ties. Work 2 rounds of surface crochet around 3rd wrist round working ties as given. **

Shape thumb:
Place working loop back on hook and cont in A.
Inc round 1: (RS) ch3, skip st at base of ch, 1dc in each of next 26 sts, 2dc in next st, 1dc in each of next 2 sts, 2dc in next st, 1dc in each of rem 19 sts, join with a sl st in top of 3ch, turn. 2 sts inc.
Patt 1 round.
Inc round 2: ch3, skip st at base of ch, 1dc in each of next 26 sts, 2dc in next st, 1dc in each of next 4 sts, 2dc in next st, 1dc in each of rem 19 sts, join with a sl st in top of 3ch, turn. 2 sts inc. Patt 1 round.
Inc round 3: ch3, skip st at base of ch, 1dc in each of next 26 sts, 2dc in next st, 1dc in each of next 6 sts, 2dc in next st, 1dc in each of rem 19 sts, join with a sl st in top of 3ch, turn. 2 sts inc.
Patt 1 round.
Cont to inc in this way on next 4 RS rounds, working 2 extra sts between incs on each round. 64 sts.
Next round: (WS) ch1, 1sc in same place as sl st, 1sc in each of next 20 sts, 2ch, skip next 16 sts for thumb opening,

1sc in each of rem 27 sts, join with a sl st in first sc, turn.
***Next round: ch3, skip st at base of ch, 1dc in each sc and each of the 2ch at thumb opening, join with a sl st in top of 3ch, turn. 50 sts.
Patt 6 rounds.

Little finger:
Round 1: (WS) ch1, 1sc in same place as sl st, 1sc in each of next 4 sts, ch3, skip 40 sts, 1sc in each of last 5 sts, join with a sl st in first sc, turn.
Round 2: ch3, skip st at base of ch, 1dc in each of next 5 sts, 1dc in each of 3ch, 1dc in each of next 4 sts, join with a sl st in top of 3ch, turn. 13 sts.
Patt 7 rounds.
Last round: ch3, skip st at base of ch, (dc3tog) 4 times, join with a sl st in top of 3ch. 5 sts. Fasten off.

Ring finger:
Round 1: With WS facing, rejoin A to first of 3ch at base of little finger, ch1, 1sc in same place as join, dc2tog over next 2ch, 1sc in each of next 6 sts, ch3, skip 28 sts, 1sc in each of next 6 sts, join with a sl st in first sc, turn.
Round 2: ch3, skip st at base of ch, 1dc in each of next 6 sts, 1dc in next ch, dc2tog over next 2ch, 1dc in each of next 7 sts, join with a sl st in top of 3ch, turn. 16 sts.
Patt 9 rounds.
Last round: ch3, skip st at base of ch, (dc3tog) 5 times, join with a sl st in top of 3ch. 6 sts. Fasten off.

Middle finger:
Round 1: With WS facing, rejoin A to first of 3ch at base of ring finger, ch1, 1sc in same place as join, sc2tog over next 2ch, 1sc in each of next 7 sts, ch3, skip 14 sts, 1sc in each of next 7 sts, join with a sl st in first sc, turn.
Round 2: ch3, skip st at base of ch, 1dc in each of next 7 sts, 1dc in next ch, dc2tog over next 2ch, 1dc in each of next 8 sts, join with a sl st in top of 3ch, turn. 18 sts.
Patt 11 rounds.
Last round: ch3, skip st at base of ch, dc2tog, (tr3tog) 5 times, join with a sl st in top of 3ch. 7 sts. Fasten off.

Index finger:
Round 1: With WS facing, rejoin A to first of 3ch at base of middle finger, ch1, 1sc in same place as join, sc2tog over next 2ch, 1sc in each of next 14 sts, join with a sl st in first sc, turn. 16 sts.
Patt 10 rounds.
Last round: ch3, skip st at base of ch, (dc3tog) 5 times, join with a sl st in top of 3ch. 6 sts. Fasten off.

Thumb:
With WS facing, rejoin A to first of 2ch of thumb opening, ch1, 1sc in same place as join, 1sc in next ch, 1sc

in each of 16 sts, join with a sl st in first sc, turn. 18 sts.
Patt 8 rounds.
Last round: ch3, skip st at base of ch, dc2tog, (dc3tog) 5 times, join with a sl st in top of 3ch. 7 sts. Fasten off.

Top rib:
With smaller hook and RS facing, join A around ch3 at beg of Patt round 1 at top edge, working over the Foundation round work, ch3, (inserting hook from front and from right to left, work 1dc around stem of next dc, inserting hook from back and from right to left, work 1dc around stem of foll dc) to last st, inserting hook from front and from right to left, work 1dc around stem of next dc, join with a sl st in top of 3ch. Fasten off.

LEFT GLOVE:
Work as given for Right Glove to **.
Shape thumb:
Place working loop of A back on hook.
Inc round 1: (RS) ch3, skip st at base of ch, 1dc in each of next 18 sts, 2dc in next st, 1dc in each of next 2 sts, 2dc in next st, 1dc in each of rem 27 sts, join with a sl st in top of 3ch, turn. 2 sts inc.
Patt 1 round.
Inc round 2: ch3, skip st at base of ch, 1dc in each of next 18 sts, 2dc in next st, 1dc in each of next 4 sts, 2dc in next st, 1dc in each of rem 27 sts, join with a sl st in top of 3ch, turn. 2 sts inc.
Patt 1 round.
Inc round 3: ch3, skip st at base of ch, 1dc in each of next 18 sts, 2dc in next st, 1dc in each of next 6 sts, 2dc in next st, 1dc in each of rem 27 sts, join with sl st in top of 3ch, turn. 2 sts inc.
Patt 1 round.
Cont to inc in this way on next 4 RS rounds, working 2 extra sts between incs on each round. 64 sts.
Next round: (WS) ch1, 1sc in same place as sl st, 1sc in each of next 28 sts, ch2, skip next 16 sts for thumb opening, 1sc in each of rem 19 sts, join with a sl st in first sc, turn.
Complete as given for Right Glove from ***.

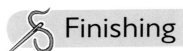 Finishing

Darn in all ends. Press lightly. Make a single knot in each pair of ties.

Oversized chevron hat

You'll turn heads when you wear this amazing slouchy hat.

This big, baggy hat has a rib-effect headband and an attractive chevron pattern in colorful stripes. The multicolor pom pom adds the finishing touch.

GETTING STARTED

Pattern is simple to follow once the chevrons appear.

Size:
To fit an average-sized woman's head with circumference of approximately 22 inches (56cm)

How much yarn:
2 x 50g (1¾oz) balls of King Cole Merino Blend DK in color A—Graphite (shade 702)
1 ball in each of 3 other colors: B—Oatmeal (shade 41); C—Scarlet (shade 9) and D—Olive (shade 69)

Hooks:
3.50mm (E/4) crochet hook
4.00mm (G/6) crochet hook

Additional items:
Sewing needle and matching thread
Piece of cardboard or pom pom maker (optional)

Gauge:
12 sts (1 patt) measure 2¾ inches (7cm) over chevron patt on 4.00mm (G/6) hook
IT IS ESSENTIAL TO WORK TO THE STATED GAUGE TO ACHIEVE SUCCESS.

What you have to do:
Work headband first in one color and rows of half double crochet worked into front or back loop only of stitches to resemble ribbing. Pick up stitches for main part of hat from one long edge of headband. Work main pattern in double crochet and stripes of chevron pattern, shaping as directed. Make pom pom and sew to top of hat.

The Yarn
King Cole Merino Blend DK (approx. 112m/122 yards per 50g/1¾oz ball) is 100% pure wool in a practical superwash format. It makes an attractive fabric, and there is a wide color range.

Instructions

Abbreviations:

alt = alternate
ch = chain(s)
cm = centimeter(s)
dc = double crochet
dc2(4)tog = work 1tr into next 2(4) sts as directed leaving last loop of each on hook, yo and draw through all 3(5) loops on hook
dec = decrease
foll = follow(s)(ing)
hdc = half double crochet
mm = millimeter(s)
patt = pattern
rep = repeat
RS = right side
sp = space
st(s) = stitch(es)
yo = yarn over hook

Note:

When working main part of Hat, always join in new color on last part of last st in old color. Work over tail of old color for about 2 inches (5cm) to enclose it, but leave a 6 inch (15cm) tail of new color to use when joining seam.

HAT:

Headband:

With smaller hook and A, ch16.

Foundation row: (RS) 1hdc into 3rd ch from hook, 1hdc into each ch to end, turn. 15 sts.

Row 1: ch2 (counts as first hdc), skip st at base of ch, 1hdc into front loop only of each hdc to end, working last hdc in 2nd of 2ch, turn.

Row 2: ch2, skip st at base of ch, 1hdc into back loop only of each hdc to end, working last hdc in 2nd of 2ch, turn.

Rep last 2 rows 34 more times, then work Row 1 again. 72 rows in all. Fasten off. With larger hook and RS of Headband facing, join B at right-hand end of one long edge.

Row 1: ch1 (counts as first sc), 1sc into side edge of each row to end, turn. 73 sts.

Row 2: ch3 (counts as first dc), 1dc into st at base of ch, *1dc into each of next 7sc, (1dc, ch1, 1dc) into next sc, rep from * to last 8 sts, 1dc into each of next 7sc, 2tr into ch1, turn. 91 sts.

Row 3: ch3, 1dc into st at base of ch, *1dc into each of next 9dc, (1dc, ch1, 1dc) into ch1 sp, rep from * to last 10 sts,

1dc into each of next 9dc, 2dc into 3rd of 3ch, turn. 109 sts. Fasten off B and join in C.

Patt row: ch3, 1dc into first dc, *1dc into each of next 4dc, dc2tog over (next and foll alt dc), 1dc into each of next 4dc, (1dc, ch1, 1dc) into 1ch sp, rep from * to last 12 sts, 1dc into each of next 4dc, dc2tog as set, 1dc into each of next 4dc, 2dc into 3rd of 3ch, turn. Fasten off C. Rep Patt row throughout in color sequence as foll: 2 rows A, 1 row D, 1 row B, 2 rows C, 1 row A, 1 row D, 2 rows B, 1 row C, 1 row A, and 1 row D. Do not fasten off D.

Shape top:

Dec row 1: With D, ch3, skip st at base of ch, *1dc into each of next 4dc, dc2tog as set, 1dc into each of next 4dc, skip 1ch sp, rep from * to last 12 sts, 1dc into each of next 4dc, dc2tog as set, 1dc into each of next 4dc, 1dc into 3rd of 3ch, turn. 83 sts.
Fasten off D and join in B.

Dec row 2: ch3, skip st at base of ch, *1dc into each of next 3dc, dc2tog as set, 1dc into each of next 3dc, rep from * to last st, 1dc into 3rd of 3ch, turn. 65 sts.
Fasten off B and join in C.

Dec row 3: ch3, skip st at base of ch, *1dc into next dc, tr4tog over (first, 2nd, 4th, and 5th foll dc), 1dc into next dc, rep from * to last st, 1dc into 3rd of 3ch. 29 sts.
Fasten off leaving a long tail.

 ## Finishing

Starting at lower edge, join back seam using yarn tails to match each stripe. Thread final yarn tail into needle and run in and out along top edge, gather up tightly, and backstitch securely to close. Using all 4 colors, make a pom pom about 2¾ inches (7cm) in diameter (see Finishing instructions on page 63) and sew to gathered top of hat.

Zigzag scarf

A simple stitch worked in increases and decreases gives the chevron-shape to this scarf.

This chevron-pattern scarf, worked in double crochet and graduated shades of one color, makes a striking accessory to liven up your wardrobe.

GETTING STARTED

Easy pattern to follow once the foundation row has been established.

Size:
Scarf measures 5 x 52 inches (13 x 132cm), excluding fringe.

How much yarn:
1 x 50g (1¾oz) ball of Debbie Bliss Baby Cashmerino in each of 4 colors: A—Peppermint Green (shade 003); B—Pale Green (shade 002); C—Aqua Green (shade 040) and D—Dark Turquoise (shade 203)

Hook:
4.00mm (G/6) crochet hook

Gauge:
10 sts (1 patt rep) measure 2⅜ inches (6cm) and 4 rows (1 patt rep) measure 1½ inches (4cm) on 4.00mm (G/6) hook
IT IS ESSENTIAL TO WORK TO THE STATED GAUGE TO ACHIEVE SUCCESS.

What you have to do:
Make long length of foundation chain. Work throughout in double crochet, creating chevron pattern by mass increasing and decreasing stitches at intervals throughout each row. Work each row in a different color. Knot matching tassels into row ends.

The Yarn
Debbie Bliss Cashmerino DK (approx. 110m/120 yards per 50g/1¾oz ball) contains 55% merino wool, 33% microfiber and 12% cashmere. It is extremely soft, can be machine washed and there is a wide palette of beautiful colors is available.

Instructions

Abbreviations:

ch = chain(s)

cm = centimeter(s)

dc = double crochet

dc3tog = work 1dcin each of next 3 sts leaving last loop of each on hook, yarn round hook and draw through all 4 loops

mm = millimeter(s)

patt = pattern

rep = repeat

RS = right side

st(s) = stitch(es)

yo = yarn over hook

SCARF:

With A, ch224 loosely.

Foundation row: (RS) With A, 1dc into 4th ch from hook, *1dc into each of next ch3, over next ch3 work dc3tog, 1dc into each of next ch3, 3dc into next ch, rep from * ending last rep with 2dc into last ch and joining in B for final part of last st, turn. 221 sts.

Patt row: With B, ch3 (counts as first dc), 1dc into first st at base of 3ch, *1dc into each of next 3dc, over next 3 sts work dc3tog, 1dc into each of next 3dc, 3dc into next dc, rep from * ending last rep with 2dc into top of 3ch and joining in C for final part of last st, turn. Rep last row throughout to form patt, working in stripe sequence of 1 row C, 1 row D, (1 row each A, B, C, and D) twice, then 1 row A (13 rows in all). Fasten off.

Tassels:

Cut 5 x 12 inch (30cm) lengths of yarn for each tassel. Knot a tassel into each row end across short ends of Scarf, matching stripe and tassel colors. Trim tassels evenly.

HOW TO
WORK THE PATTERN

The pattern is formed by increasing and decreasing stitches at regular intervals through the row.

1 Make a foundation chain of 224 chains. To work the foundation row, begin with one double crochet into the fourth chain from the hook.
Begin the repeat sequence by working one double into each of the next 3 chains.

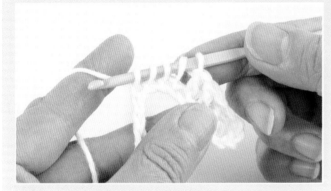

2 Now work 3 double crochets together into the next 3 chains. To do this, work one double into each of the 3 chains, leaving the last loop of each on the hook, then take the yarn over the hook and draw it through all 4 loops.

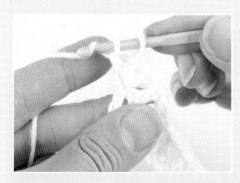

3 Work one double into each of the next 3 chains and then 3 doubles into the next chain to complete the sequence. Repeat this sequence, ending the last repeat with 2 doubles into the last chain and then joining in the new color for the last part of the stitch. Turn the work.

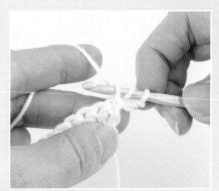

4 Chain 3 (this counts as the first double crochet) and work one double into the first stitch at the base of the turning chain.

5 Begin the repeat sequence with one double crochet into each of the next 3 stitches. Over the next 3 stitches work 3 doubles together, one double into each of the next 3 doubles and 3 doubles into the next stitch.

6 Repeat this sequence, ending the last repeat with 2 doubles into the top of the turning chain and joining in the next color for the final part of the last stitch. Turn the work.

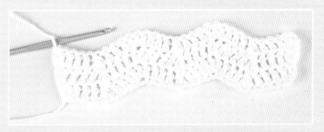

7 Repeat the last row throughout to form the pattern, changing colors as instructed.

Star pin cushion

Practice your colorwork with this mini project.

Styled as an envelope with a back button fastening and worked in single crochet, this neat pincushion has a bold star motif on the front.

GETTING STARTED

★ ★ *Working color designs by the intarsia method requires a lot of practice but this is a small design with little shaping.*

Size:
Approximately 4 inches (10cm) square

How much yarn:
1 x 50g (1¾oz) ball of Anchor Style Creativa Fino in each of 2 colors: A—White (shade 01331) and B—Red (shade 01333)

Hook:
2.50mm (B/1) crochet hook

Additional items:
5 bobbins
1 red button
2 x 4¼ inches (11cm) squares of white lining fabric
Red and white sewing thread and needle
Polyester fiberfill

Gauge:
26 sts and 30 rows measure 4 inches (10cm) square over sc on 2.50mm (B/1) hook
IT IS ESSENTIAL TO WORK TO THE STATED GAUGE TO ACHIEVE SUCCESS.

What you have to do:
Work in single crochet throughout. Work star motif on front using intarsia technique and working with small, separate lengths of yarn. Make polyester-filled fabric pad for inside pincushion.

The Yarn
Anchor Style Creativa Fino (approx. 125m/ 136 yards per 50g/1¾oz ball) is 100% pure lightweight cotton. It produces a soft fabric with a silky sheen that makes it ideal for craft projects. There is a wide range of colors.

Instructions

Abbreviations:

ch = chain(s)

cm = centimeter(s)

cont = continue

dec = decreased

foll = follows

patt = pattern

rem = remain

rep = repeat

RS = right side

sc = single crochet

sc2tog = (insert hook in next st, yo and draw a loop through) twice, yo and draw through all 3 loops on hook

sl st = slip stitch

st(s) = stitch(es)

WS = wrong side

yo = yarn over hook

Notes:

• Before you begin, cut 3 x 3-yard (3 meter-) lengths of A and wind on to individual bobbins. Also cut two x 2-yard (2 meter-) lengths of B and wind onto individual bobbins.

• When changing color, complete last part of last stitch in old color with new color. To work out which bobbin to use, pick up yarn nearest to stitch being worked.

• When working in intarsia patt, do not carry yarns across back of work. Instead use individual bobbins as stated for each area of color, twisting yarns together on WS of work when changing color to prevent a hole from forming.

FRONT:

With A, ch26.

Foundation row: (WS) 1sc in 2nd ch from hook, 1sc in each ch to end, turn. 26 sts.

Rows 1 and 2: ch1 (counts as first sc), skip first st, 1sc in each sc to end, working last sc in turning ch, turn.

Cont in sc as set, working intarsia patt as foll:

Row 3: (RS) 4 A, join on bobbin in B, 2 B, join on bobbin in A, 14 A, join on bobbin in B, 2 B, join on bobbin in A, 4 A, turn.

Row 4: 4 A, 3 B, 12 A, 2 B, 5 A, turn.

Row 5: 5 A, 3 B, 10 A, 3 B, 5 A, turn.

Row 6: 6 A, 3 B, 8 A, 3 B, 6 A, turn.

Row 7: 6 A, 4 B, 6 A, 4 B, 6 A, turn.

Row 8: 6 A, 4 B, 5 A, 4 B, 7 A, turn.

Row 9: 7 A, 4 B, 4 A, 4 B, 7 A, turn.

Row 10: 7 A, 5 B, 2 A, 4 B, 8 A, turn.

Rows 11–13: 8 A, 10 B, 8 A, turn.

Row 14: 7 A, 12 B, 7 A, turn.

Row 15: 6 A, 15 B, 5 A, turn.

Row 16: 4 A, 18 B, 4 A, turn.

Row 17: 3 A, 21 B, 2 A, turn.

Row 18: 2 A, 22 B, 2 A, turn.

Row 19: 10 A, join on bobbin in B, 6 B, join on bobbin in A, 10 A.

Row 20: 10 A, 5 B, 11 A, turn.

Row 21: 11 A, 4 B, 11 A, turn.

Row 22: 11 A, 3 B, 12 A, turn.

Row 23: 12 A, 2 B, 12 A, turn.

Row 24: 12 A, 1 B, 13 A, turn.

Row 25: 13 A, 1 B, 12 A, turn.

Row 26: As 24th.

Rows 27–29: With A only, work 3 rows in sc. Fasten off.

BACK:
Lower section:
With A, ch26. Work Foundation row as given for Front, then work 20 rows in sc.
Next row: Sl st in each st to end. Fasten off.
Top flap:
With A, ch26. Work Foundation row as given for Front,

then work 6 rows in sc.
Next row: ch1 (counts as first sc), skip first st, 1sc in each sc to last 2 sts, sc2tog over last 2 sts, turn.
1 st dec at end of row.
Rep last row until 18 sts rem.
Next row: Sl st in each of first 5 sts, ch7, skip next 7 sts, sl st in each st to end. Fasten off.

 ## Finishing

With WS facing, slipstitch front and back sections together around outer edges. Sew button to lower section of back to match chain loop.
Pincushion pad:
With RS facing, sew around edges of cotton squares, taking ¼ inch (5mm) seam allowance and leaving a small gap for turning through. Turn RS out and stuff firmly with polyester fiberfill. Neatly slipstitch opening closed. Insert pad into cover and close with button.

Beach duffle bag

Swing into summer with this brightly colored
bag over one shoulder.

Combining broad and narrow stripes in a colorful fabric, this bag, with its drawstring top, is ideal for the beach. The interior has a simple sewn lining to make it practical and sturdy.

GETTING STARTED

Bag is worked in an easy stitch pattern, but finishing requires simple sewing skills for a good finish.

Size:
Finished bag is 10¼ inches (26cm) in diameter across base x 17 inches (43cm) high

How much yarn:
1 x 100g (3½oz) ball of King Cole Bamboo Cotton DK in each of 4 colors: A—Green (shade 533; B—Peacock (shade 531); C—White (shade 530); D—Fuchsia (shade 536)

Hook:
4.00mm (G/6) crochet hook

Additional items:
⅞ yard (80cm) of 36-inch (90-cm) wide cotton fabric for lining
10-inch (25-cm) square of heavyweight iron-on interfacing
Sewing needle and thread in white and color to match lining fabric

Gauge:
19 sts measure 4 inches (10cm) and 8 rows measure 2¾ inches (7cm) over patt on sides of bag on 4.00mm (G/6) hook
IT IS ESSENTIAL TO WORK TO THE STATED GAUGE TO ACHIEVE SUCCESS.

What you have to do:
Work base of bag in rounds of half double crochet, increasing as directed. Work sides in rounds of half double crochet pattern and stripes. Make eyelet holes for drawstring. Work pocket and straps in rows of single crochet. Sew fabric lining for bag and straps.

The Yarn
King Cole Bamboo Cotton DK (approx. 230m/251 yards per 100g/3½oz ball) contains 50% cotton and 50% bamboo. It makes a soft, strong fabric with clear stitch definition. There is a good range of colors.

Instructions

Abbreviations:

beg = beginning
ch = chain
cm = centimeter(s)
cont = continue
foll = follow(s)(ing)
hdc = half double crochet
inc = increase
patt = pattern
rep = repeat
RS = right side
sc = single crochet
sl st = slip stitch
st(s) = stitch(es)
WS = wrong side

BAG:
With A, ch3.
Round 1: 8hdc in 3rd ch from hook, join with a sl st in top of first hdc.
Round 2: ch2 (do not count as a st), 2hdc in st at base of ch, 2hdc in each st to end, join with a sl st in top of first hdc. 16 sts.
Round 3: ch2, 1hdc in st at base of ch, (2hdc in next st, 1hdc in next st) 7 times, 2hdc in last st, join with a sl st in top of first hdc. 24 sts.
Round 4: ch2, 1hdc in st at base of ch, 1hdc in next st, (2hdc in next st, 1hdc in each of next 2 sts) 7 times, 2hdc in last st, join with a sl st in top of first hdc. 32 sts.
Round 5: ch2, 1hdc in st at base of ch, 1hdc in each of next 2 sts, (2hdc in next st, 1hdc in each of next 3 sts) 7 times, 2hdc in last st, join with a sl st in top of first hdc.

40 sts.
Round 6: ch2, 1hdc in st at base of ch, 1hdc in each of next 3 sts, (2hdc in next st, 1hdc in each of next 4 sts) 7 times, 2hdc in last st, join with a sl st in top of first hdc. 48 sts.
Cont in rounds as set, working 1 extra st between each inc, until foll round has been worked: "ch2, 1hdc in st at base of ch, 1hdc in each of next 12 sts, (2hdc in next st, 1hdc in each of next 13 sts) 7 times, 2hdc in last st, join with a sl st in top of first hdc. 120 sts."
Next round: ch2, 1hdc in st at base of ch, 1hdc in each st to end, join with a sl st in top of first hdc. Fasten off A.
Join C to same place as last sl st and cont in patt as foll:
Round 1: ch2, 1hdc in back loop only of st at base of ch, *1hdc in front loop only of next st, 1hdc in back loop only of next st,

rep from * to last st, 1hdc in front loop only of last st, join with a sl st in top of first hdc.

Round 2: ch2, 1hdc in front loop only of st at base of ch, *1hdc in back loop only of next st, 1hdc in front loop only of next st, rep from * to last st, 1hdc in back loop only of last st, join with a sl st in top of first hdc.

The last 2 rounds form patt. Cont in patt, working in stripes of 6 rounds B, 2 rounds C, 6 rounds D, 2 rounds C, 6 rounds A, 2 rounds C, 6 rounds B, 2 rounds C, and 6 rounds D.

Eyelet round: With C, ch2, 1hdc in back loop only of st at base of ch, patt 10 sts, (ch1, skip next st, patt 11 sts) 9 times, ch1, skip last st, join with a sl st in 2nd of 2ch. Patt 1 more round with C, then patt 6 rounds in A.

Last 2 rounds: With C, ch1 (does not count as a st), 1sc in each st to end, join with a sl st in first sc.
Fasten off.

STRAPS: (makes 2)

With B, ch11.

Foundation row: 1sc in 2nd ch from hook, 1sc in each ch to end, turn.

Patt row: ch1 (does not count as a st), 1sc in each st to end, turn. 10 sts. Rep last row until Strap measures 30 inches (76cm) from beg. Fasten off.

POCKET: (worked sideways)

With B, ch27. Work Foundation and Patt row as given for Straps. 26 sts. Cont in sc and stripe sequence of 4 more rows B, 2 rows C, 6 rows D, 2 rows C, 6 rows A, 2 rows C, 6 rows D, 2 rows C, and 6 rows B, always joining in new color on last part of last st in old color. Fasten off.

Edging:

With C and RS of work facing, join yarn to first row end of one edge, ch1, 1sc in each row end to corner, turn. Work 1 more row in sc. Fasten off.

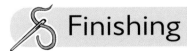

Finishing

Lining:

Cut a 10¼in- (26cm-) diameter circle from cotton fabric and a 9½in- (24cm-)diameter circle from iron-on interfacing. Apply to center of WS of fabric. Cut a piece 17¾ x 25½ inch (45 x 65cm) along the length of fabric. Taking a ⅜ inches (1cm) seam allowance, join short ends to form an open tube. Now sew interfaced circle into one end of open tube. With WS facing, slip lining inside bag.

Fold raw edge of lining to inside and slipstitch in place around top edge, just below last 2 rounds of sc.

To make casing, work a row of small, neat running sts through base of sts of eyelet round. Work another row of running sts through top of sts on round above. With white sewing thread, work a row of running stitches through the middle of each white stripe on bag.

With C, make a twisted cord about 32 inches (80cm) long. Thread cord through eyelets so that ends emerge at center front.

Sew pocket to center front of bag as shown in photograph.

Cut a length of fabric 32 inches (80cm) long and ¾ inch (2cm) wider than straps. Cut in half widthwise. Turn in raw edges of one piece and slipstitch in place to one end of strap, ending at center. Turn strap over and sew second piece to other end of strap.

Sew center of strap securely to center back of bag, just below casing. Sew loose ends of straps securely to base of bag, approximately 8 inches (20cm) apart.

Index

Acknowledgments

Managing Editor: Clare Churly
Editors: Lesley Malkin and Eleanor van Zandt
Senior Art Editor: Juliette Norsworthy
Designer: Janis Utton
Production Controller: Allison Gonsalves